To Pastor Ted Breuckner

May God's best be
yours. Thanks for
good fellowship at
camp seeley. Gal 6:9.

Maynard Force

D0894845

JONAH SPEAKS

JONAH SPEAKS

DEVOTIONAL MEDITATIONS
FROM THE BOOK OF JONAH

by

MAYNARD A. FORCE
TEACHER, LUTHERAN BIBLE INSTITUTE

THE LUTHERAN BIBLE INSTITUTE
1619 PORTLAND AVENUE, MINNEAPOLIS 4, MINNESOTA

Printed and Manufactured in the United States of America
by Augsburg Publishing House, Minneapolis, Minnesota

Dedicated to my wife, whose tender love and affection, whose kind and sympathetic understanding in Christ Jesus have been a constant and enriching source of inspiration.

CONTENTS

Chapter III. REVIVAL

Chapter IV. REBELLION

Introduction

Meet the Prophet Jonah

Apart from what we find in the book of Jonah itself, our information about the prophet Jonah is very limited. He is mentioned in just a few other places in the Bible.

Jonah must have lived about the year 800 B.C., either during or just previous to the reign of King Jeroboam II of Israel. He is referred to in II Kings 14:25 as the prophet who foretold the victories of this king. He prophesied that Jeroboam would "restore the border of Israel from the entrance of Hannath unto the sea Arabah." The fact that Jonah's prophecy came true proves that he was a true prophet according to the requirement stated in Jeremiah: "When the word of the prophet shall come to pass, then shall the prophet be known, that Jehovah hath truly sent him" (28:9)

Jonah lived at a time of great wickedness. Though Jeroboam II was a victorious king, he "did that which was evil in the sight of Jehovah" (II Kings 14:24). Wickedness was increasing in Israel, and the false prophets were the popular men of the day. It was a matter of only a few years after Jonah's appearance that Israel was ripe for judgment. In these twilight hours of Israel's history, Jonah made his appearance as one of God's representatives.

Jonah was God's mouthpiece in those days. We read, "The word of Jehovah, the God of Israel, which he spake by his servant Jonah, the son of Amittai, the prophet, who was of Gath-hepher" (II Kings 14:25). Notice that he had the honor of being a servant of Jehovah—a chosen representative of the living God. Furthermore, he spoke the word of Jehovah. Even in those times of wickedness, God's word was heard through Jonah. He was also highly honored with the title prophet. In spite of all Jonah's weaknesses he had been chosen of God to be a light in a dark place.

It is interesting to note that even though Israel was in a sad state of affairs spiritually, God called one of its few remaining lights to carry the message to foreign lands. The old argument that "we need to stay at home and preach because of the great need" does not correspond with the Lord's method of doing things. When the light was going out in Israel, God chose Jonah to take it to Assyria. Only one verse in Scripture tells us of Jonah's work at home, while the entire book of Jonah tells of his call and work elsewhere.

Jesus referred to Jonah at least twice (Matt. 12: 39-41; 16:4; and Luke 11:29-32). When the scribes and Pharisees were seeking after a sign, he abruptly answered: "An evil and adulterous generation seeketh after a sign; and there shall no sign be given to it but the sign of Jonah the prophet: for as Jonah was three days and three nights in the belly of the whale; so shall the Son of Man be three days and three nights in the heart of the earth. The men of Nineveh shall stand up in the judgment with this generation, and shall condemn it: for they repented at the preaching of Jonah; and behold, a greater than Jonah is here" (Matt. 12:39-41; 16:4). In

Luke this thought is added: "For even as Jonah became a sign unto the Ninevites, so shall also the Son of man be to this generation" (11:30). It is interesting to notice that Jesus referred to Jonah's experience as a past fact which He expected His hearers to know about. The sign, then some 800 years old, was still good and it was verified by Jesus himself. Christ compared the fact that He would have to spend three days and three nights in the heart of the earth to that of Jonah's experience of spending three days and three nights in the belly of the fish. Jesus would not have given such an important place to Jonah if he had not been an important Old Testament prophet.

The name Jonah means dove. He was to be as peaceful as the most gentle of birds; but, when we follow him through his book, we find his life to be one of turmoil. As in the case of many others, his life did not correspond with his name. Zaccheus, the man who climbed a tree to see Jesus, had been given a name that meant pure, but his life was anything but pure until he was converted. Of the church in Sardis Jesus said, "Thou hast a name that thou livest, and thou art dead" (Rev. 3:1). Many people bear the name Christian but live a life definitely contrary to that name.

The purpose of this introduction is to acquaint you with a man whom you should learn to know better The book of Jonah with but four short chapters centers itself around this servant of God and brings lessons full of eternal blessings. With these few introductory remarks, we invite you to join us in a devotional study of the book

1

"Now"

> "Now the word of Jehovah came unto Jonah" (Jonah 1:1).

The book of Jonah, according to most versions, begins with the word "now." We shall use this word as it pertains to the time element and let it serve as a door through which we enter this book.

There is an entire sermon hidden away in this one word "now." It is used throughout the entire Bible and is especially significant when connected with God's promises. Let us meditate for a few moments on this word.

It is always so easy to postpone accepting God's promises, thinking we shall accept them at some future date. To be sure, there are many promises that will be fulfilled in the future, but remember *all* of God's promises are for us. God has something for us right now, this very day, these moments when we are reading these very lines.

The word "now" should be of supreme importance to all seeking souls. The Lord has plainly shown us from His word that *now* is the time for salvation. "Behold now is the acceptable time, behold now is the day of salvation" (II Cor. 6:2). It is interesting to know that in this emphatic invitation the word "now" is found two times. The Lord knows our weaknesses and would remind us not to fritter away the present opportunities. It is foolish, then, to interpret the word "now" to mean tomorrow or next year. The Lord knows how many times we miss great blessings just because we fail to heed this simple word "now."

The Lord's time is "now." His invitation reads: "All things are now ready" (Luke 14:17). Jesus has already atoned for sin by giving His life on the cross. He will not die again for any man, for "he died once and for all." Salvation is therefore free to all who will accept it. A seeking sinner need not try to persuade God to work out another plan of salvation, for God's only plan has been carried out to perfection. Jesus Christ has already "tasted death for every man." Therefore, the Lord can say all things are "now" ready. Salvation is yours now for the taking.

The word "now" is also a great blessing to all struggling souls. God's word plainly states, "There is therefore now no condemnation to them that are in Christ Jesus" (Rom. 8:1). This promise would mean more to us if we would study its setting. Remember the seventh chapter of Romans is the struggling chapter that leads to this glorious verse. In the original copy of the Bible there were no chapter or verse divisions. Therefore, the apostle Paul's heart-cry, "Wretched man that I am, who shall deliver me out of the body of this death" (Rom. 7:24), is also answered by this glorious promise. Isn't it wonderful to know that there is therefore "now" no condemnation for those who are trusting in Jesus for salvation? To be sure, the

5

devil may work on your feelings so that you may feel condemned, but God's Word states otherwise. When it is a choice between your feelings or God's Word, pray for grace to base your hope on the unchangeable Word of God. If the word "now" had not been in this promise, we might have been tempted to believe that in some distant day there would be no condemnation for the believers. How thankful we should be for this one word "now"!

The word "now" carries with it a special blessing to all who are established Christians. John wrote to the believers in his day, "Beloved, now are we children of God" (I John 3:2). This makes it plain that we carry the distinguished honor of being children of God "now." Some would be prone to be tempted to believe that such an honor can be bestowed only on the saints in heaven. For that reason we have just such a verse. We do not need to wait until we stand before the judgment seat of God to find out about our standing with Him, for "The Spirit himself beareth witness with our spirit that we are children of God" (Rom. 8:16). Let us therefore lay claim to all that is ours now.

This little word "now" is like a key. To be sure, it is small for it contains only three letters . . . but all keys are small compared to the rooms that they can unlock. It seems that Jehovah is handing us a key. at the very outset of our study in this book and is telling us to use it. Whoever we are or whatever our spiritual condition may be, let us pray for grace to understand what the Lord means when He says "now." Then we can pray with the saints of old, "This is the day which Jehovah hath made; we will rejoice and be glad in it. Save *now*, we beseech thee, Send *now* prosperity" (Psalm 118:24, 25).

2

The Importance of the Word

"The word of Jehovah" (Jonah 1:1).

The book of Jonah introduces us immediately to the phrase "the word of Jehovah." In this instance it refers to the specific word that reached Jonah to "arise, go and . . . cry." Usually when we speak of "the word of Jehovah," we mean the revealed word of God as we have it recorded in the Bible. Before entering further into the book of Jonah, let us consider a few facts about the word of Jehovah.

The Word of God produces life. Peter explained to the Christians of his day that they had life "having been begotten again [born again] not of corruptible seed, but of the incorruptible through the word of God which liveth and abideth" (I Peter 1:23). Our physical birth came as a result of the seed of our parent; but our second birth comes through the incorruptible seed, God's word. He that would have spiritual life must then receive it through the Word.

The Word of God provides the light for our daily walk. The Psalmist affirmed, "Thy word is a lamp unto my feet, and light unto my path" (Ps. 119: 105). He knew the value of God's word. He, like the rest of the saints, had carefully made his way around the pitfalls of life by means of this light. Many a weary soul who has come to a standstill has been able to proceed only after the light of God's word has been shed on his way. Friend, has the pathway of your life become darkened by suspicions, doubts and fears? Do you feel that you have come to the end of the road? Are you wondering what to do next? Then use God's word freely for it has been given you for that purpose. Remember that "the opening of thy words giveth light" (Ps. 119:130).

God's word is forever established in heaven. "Forever, O Jehovah, thy word is settled in heaven" (Ps. 119:89). Once God's word proceeds out of his mouth, no one in heaven ever doubts it. It is forever settled there. It is too bad this same Word cannot be forever settled in our hearts. How different our lives would be if that were so. There would then be some great changes taking place. As the Word becomes established in our hearts, it creates faith which gives victory over temptation and banishes doubt, worry, fear and other related sins.

The word of God will never fail. God himself has promised, "I watch over my word to perform it" (Jer. 1:2). This Word has stood the test of time, and it can be said of it that "every word of God is tried" (Prov. 30:5). It can never be changed for God has affirmed, "My covenant will I not break nor alter the thing that is gone out of my lips" (Ps. 89:34). Changing times have no effect upon it. "Heaven and earth shall pass away but my word shall not pass away" (Matt. 24:35). No revolutionary changes that take place in this world will change it for "one jot or one tittle shall in no wise pass away from the law, till all things be accomplished"

(Matt. 5:18). It is good to know that there is one thing on earth today that will weather the storms of time. May this never failing Word strengthen your faith so that you may be "rooted and builded up in him, and established in your faith, even as ye were taught abounding in thanksgiving" (Col. 2:7).

Since "the word of Jehovah" is so important, let us approach it reverently. It is no common thing but rather a valuable inheritance that has been handed us. Never read the Word without first praying that the Holy Spirit may be your teacher. He is ready to "guide you into all the truth" (John 16:13), for "he shall teach you all things" (John 14:26). Beware of handling the Word in a mechanical way; the many who do that receive no blessing. The Word to them seems dry and even boring. The only way to study the Word is first to pray sincerely, "Open mine eyes that I may behold wondrous things out of thy law" (Ps. 119:18). Memorize this verse and make it your approaching prayer. Use it often and "the word of Jehovah" will become very precious to you.

3

The Word of God Accepted, Rejected, or ?

"The word of Jehovah came unto Jonah" (Jonah 1:1).

The word of Jehovah found its way to Jonah's heart. How this was done we are not told. It is enough for us to know that the Lord's word had reached its desired objective, and Jonah was standing face to face with God. That moment in the life of any individual is a very solemn one. It became just that for Jonah.

Blessed is the man who gives God a chance to meet him through His Word. That man stands at the threshold of great blessings. He is honored with the greatest honor that can be bestowed upon a human being. All the riches of heaven as well as all the true joys of earth are before him. The most interesting chapter of his life is ready to begin.

They that accept the Word and are obedient to it are overwhelmed at its blessings. One man testified, "I love thy commandments above gold, yea, above fine gold" (Ps. 119:127). In other words, he meant that the word of God was more precious to him than thousands of dollars, yea, than millions of dollars. Do you feel that way about God's word? Some people say that, but they do not mean it. If they meant it, they would read the Bible more often, gladly hear it preached, and would do their utmost to give it out to others. Then their desires for material things would fade as their desire for the Word increased.

Job had come to realize the blessings of God's word when he said, "I have treasured up the words of his mouth more than my necessary food" (Job 23:12). That is a startling statement. Job enjoyed the word of God more than eating. How many people can you find like that today? If Job could discover the preciousness of God's word, should not we be able to rediscover it today? The day of discoveries is not over yet. If it is adventure you crave, "search the Scriptures."

They that neglect the Word are doomed to damnation. Most neglectors do not realize that; but just a statement or two from God's word should convince them. The question is asked, "How shall we escape, if we neglect so great a salvation?" (Heb. 2: 3). This question has no answer because there is no escape. Therefore, "see that ye refuse not him that speaketh. For if they escaped not when they refused him that warned them on earth, much more shall not we escape who turn away from him that warneth from heaven" (Heb. 12:25).

The Bible is full of examples of those who once had free access to God's word but who lost out completely because they did not obey it. The people of Judah were doomed to captivity because they had "rejected the law of Jehovah and have not kept his statutes" (Amos 2:4). King Saul was told he would lose his kingdom because he had "not kept the commandment of Jehovah" (I Sam. 13:13). Jehovah said through the prophet Jeremiah, "I will bring evil upon this people . . . because they have not hearkened unto my words and as for my law, they have rejected it" (Jer. 6:19). In our day, too, countless examples could be given of those who are doomed to hell for this same reason.

Possibly you have neither neglected nor rejected God's word, but neither have you actually accepted it. Then you are guilty of abusing it. This is commonly done for the word of Jehovah can very easily be mistreated. Some of us have heard it so often that there is a danger of its becoming common place. We are in danger of treating this heavenly manna as the Israelites treated the manna in the wilderness when they said, "Our soul loatheth this light bread" (Numbers 21:5). Fiery serpents immediately were sent as a judgment to kill many of the people. Our ranks, too, have been thinned because of the twentieth century serpents that have come as judgment upon those who despise the Word. Poisonous serpents of every worldly variety have glided into our congregations and homes, leaving death and destruction in their wake. It is a serious offense against God when we no longer enjoy His word. "Whoso despiseth the word bringeth destruction on himself" (Prov. 13:13). From the time we lose our appetite for it until we actually loathe it is but a single step.

If this day finds you dull and indifferent towards God's word, pray! Confess this attitude as sin and pray to the Lord as David did, "Create in me a clean heart, O God; and renew a right spirit within me" (Ps. 51:10). Why continue to live a dull and drab life when the Lord has something far better for you? The living God is desirous of reaching you through His word so that He can bless and guide your life into channels of usefulness. The word of Jehovah came to Jonah facing him with a definite challenge. A similar challenge is before us if we are willing to permit the word of Jehovah to have access to our hearts. Is your heart open?

4

"Arise, Go, . . . Cry"

"Arise, go. . . . cry" (Jonah 1:2).

The Lord wanted Jonah to do a work of eternal value. He had a definite task for him to do. He therefore made it clear that the time had now come to arise, go and cry. These three words constituted the main part of his call and required his immediate attention.

ARISE. How simple! It means action. Regardless of what you are doing when this word reaches you, the time has come to arouse yourself. If you have been spiritually sleeping, listen to the alarm as it sounds: "Awake, thou that sleepest, and arise from the dead, and Christ shall shine upon thee" (Eph. 5:14). Again, hear the alarm as it quickly repeats itself, "And this, knowing the season, that already it is time for you to awake out of sleep: for now is salvation nearer to us than when we first believed. The night is far spent, and the day is at hand: let us therefore cast off the works of darkness, and let us put on the armor of light" (Rom. 13:11, 12). In other words, get up. How long will you continue your inactivity? If you have been waiting for the "go" signal, you have it here. The captain of your soul is calling, "Attention!" Arise, stand in His presence for He is ready to speak.

GO. You have been divinely chosen by the King of kings to carry out His commission. Why you should have been chosen you will never be able to reason out, and neither will anyone else. That belongs to the eternal wisdom of God. Lest you become proud, listen to our Lord describe the class of people He uses, "Behold your calling, brethren, that not many wise after the flesh, not many mighty, not many noble, are called: but GOD CHOSE THE FOOLISH things of the world, that he might put to shame them that are wise; and GOD CHOSE THE WEAK things of the world, that he might put to shame the things that are strong . . . that no flesh should glory before God" (I Cor. 1:26, 27, 29). Blessed is the man who first has been aroused and then has been willing to stand in the presence of the Lord and hear the simple word, "Go." With that short command is given all the power necessary to carry it out. The one who has been thus appointed can draw from all the resources of heaven to fulfill his commission. "Behold, I have given you authority . . . over all the power of the enemy" (Luke 10: 19), said Jesus to His disciples.

CRY. This is the third and last word of the call. When once the destination has been reached, there is something definite to do. A divine message is to be delivered. The King of kings wants His will to be made known. He that once said, "Be not anxious how or what ye shall speak; for it shall be given you in that hour what ye shall speak" (Matt. 10:19), will also give you the words to speak. Remember, "It was God's good pleasure through the foolishness of the preaching to save them that believe" (I Cor. 1:21). This is still God's simple method of saving souls today. It is wonderful that He still calls men to carry out His great work in the same way. Realizing this truth the disciples once prayed, "Grant unto thy servants to *speak thy word with all boldness,* while thou stretchest forth thy hand to heal and that signs and wonders may be done through the name of thy holy Servant Jesus" (Acts 4:29, 30). Their one request for themselves was to preach the Word boldly, for they knew the Lord would apply the Word to the hearts of the listeners.

Three simple words, arise, go and cry. First "arise." Stand in God's presence. He cannot speak until you are awake. Then listen to Him say, "Go." "Go ye therefore, and make disciples of all the nations" (Matt. 28:19). Listen the third time as He says, "Cry." "Teaching them to observe all things whatsoever I commanded you: and lo, I am with you always, even unto the end of the world" (Matt. 28:20). Pray that your spiritual ear may be tuned to hear and understand the significance of these three words.

> "Put it first—*the great commission.*
>   Put it first—*the great command.*
> Put it first—*our standing orders.*
>   Put it first—*on sea and land.*
> Put it first—*in every parish.*
>   Put it first—*in every heart.*
> Put it first—*don't put it second.*
>   God's own Bible is our chart."
>
> (Selected)

5

Go to Nineveh

"Arise, go to Nineveh, that great city, and cry against it" (Jonah 1:2).

The name Nineveh must have caused Jonah to tremble. It was the capital city of the Assyrians, who were an ungodly lot of people. The Lord characterized the city as a place of wickedness. Besides this, Nineveh belonged to Israel's enemy—their bitter and despised foe—the Assyrians. It was to this place that Jonah was told to go.

The Lord always chooses difficult places in which to do His greatest work. Jonah was sent to the very stronghold of evil. He once told Jeremiah, "Call unto me, and I will answer thee, and will show thee great things, and difficult, which thou knowest not" (Jer. 33:3). How could the Lord do difficult things unless His servants were in difficult places? The Lord's servants have always had their greatest victories where they have encountered their greatest battles.

Moses, for example, was sent to the capital of Egypt to demand from the haughty Pharaoh the freedom of the Israelites. No man ever had a more difficult mission. Elijah, the prophet, was delegated by the Lord to go to Samaria, the capital city of Israel, to face the wicked king Ahab. The apostles were told "not to depart from Jerusalem" (Acts 1: 4), that wicked city in which their Master had been condemned and crucified, but to tarry there until they were endowed with power from on high. It was in this same city that they later established the headquarters for the early Christian church. The apostle Paul was sent to Ephesus, the hotbed of heathen worship and the home of the goddess Diana, there to establish a strong Christian church. He was later sent to Rome, the capital of a world empire to secure another foothold for Christianity. These and many more examples could be sighted to show that the Lord sends His representatives to trying and challenging places.

The Lord also sends His servants to definite places. Jonah was called, not to go preaching aimlessly, but rather to bypass many cities and villages until he reached Nineveh and there cry against it.

Jesus has always led His followers to places of His own choosing. Philip the evangelist was in the midst of a mighty awakening in Samaria when he was called to "go toward the south unto the way that goeth down from Jerusalem unto Gaza" (Acts 8:26). There on that desert highway he met "a man of Ethiopia," to whom he showed the way of salvation. Had Philip gone on any other road that day, he would have missed his calling.

Ananias, the man used to help the apostle Paul find peace with God, was told, "Arise, and go to the street which is called Straight, and inquire in the house of Judas for *one* named Saul, a man of Tarsus: for behold, he prayeth" (Acts 9:11). Notice how definite God was in this particular call. No doubt Ananias passed by many people before he got to the ONE that the Lord was after. Had he spoken to a hundred other people that day and missed Paul, he would have missed his calling. There can be no substitution of places when God calls to service.

The Lord knows best where to send His servants. He is the commander-in-chief of His own army and knows who is best fitted for the various lines of duty. He therefore dispatches each servant in a very personal way.

The apostle Paul wanted to bring the gospel to Asia, but he was "forbidden of the Holy Spirit to speak the word in Asia" (Act 16:6). Doesn't such guidance cause one to sit up and take notice? He next thought of going into Bithynia, but "the Spirit of Jesus suffered them not" (Acts 16:8). Finally by a vision in the night, he heard the call, "Come over into Macedonia, and help us" (v. 9). This made it clear to Paul and his friends "that God had called us to preach the gospel unto them" (v. 10). There was a definite place to which God was calling, and not until they reached that place were they at peace in their own hearts. After that, these men of God could endure any amount of abuse, for they knew they were in the place where God wanted them. Paul once wrote, "I am filled with comfort, I overflow with joy in all our affliction" (II Cor. 7:4). Only those who are in the place designated by the Lord can speak that way.

The Lord does not lead all His servants to the same place. His plan has always been to scatter them so that they might be "the salt of the earth" and "the light of the world" (Matt. 5:13, 14). When Jesus asked Peter the arresting question, "Lovest thou me?" (John 21:15), He immediately added the admonition, "Follow me." When Peter asked about his companion, "What shall this man do?" Jesus abruptly answered, "What is that to thee? follow thou me" (v. 22). Jesus wanted Peter to know that he was to follow Him regardless of what happened to anyone else. Jesus made it clear to His disciples that they were to FOLLOW Him. "Come ye after me," He said, "and I will make you fishers of men" (Matt. 4:19). Christ would lead the way Himself. They were but to follow.

One of the great joys of serving Jesus Christ is to be personally led by Him. Jesus once said, "I know mine own, and mine own know me" (John 10:14). That personal communion is cherished by every true Christian. At another time when Christ spoke about His own He said, "They follow me" (John 10:27). It is the ambition of every true Christian simply to follow Christ wherever He may lead. Some have gone over mountain and sea to their places of service, and others again have been delegated to stay in their own home community to serve God. It is not for any Christian to choose his place of service, but just to follow Christ.

Jonah was given a Nineveh in which to testify. There was no doubt in his mind where the Lord would have him serve. Every Christian is given some definite field of service. If you know where the Lord would have you serve, pray for grace that you may be found faithful regardless of the struggles which you may meet. Just remember that the saints of old had to battle their way to their places of service too. If you do not know where the Lord would have you serve, pray with the psalmist, "Teach me thy way, O Jehovah; and lead me in a plain path, because of mine enemies" (Ps. 27:11). Then hold on to the promise of God, "I will instruct thee and teach thee in the way which thou shalt go: I will counsel thee with mine eye upon thee" (Ps. 32:8).

6

Disobedience

"But Jonah rose up to flee unto Tarshish from the presence of Jehovah" (Jonah 1:3).

Jonah was a prejudiced Jew. It was not in his line of thinking that an ungodly nation like the Assyrians should have the word of God preached to them. They were a cruel people whose wickedness was of the grossest sort. Jonah would not mind preaching any place in Israel or Judah, but his pride forbade him to go to Nineveh. Therefore in desperation he chose to flee to Tarshish. He was more bent to follow his own inclinations than do the will of Jehovah.

The quickest way "to flee from the presence of Jehovah" is to disobey His Word. All who do so find themselves on the highway of disobedience. This is the devil's short-cut from God. It is always full of fast fleeing people. It has no traffic hours, for day and night it is crowded with people all hurrying in the same direction. There is no class distinction on this road, for people of all walks of life are found here. Jonah was as one of these—a prospective preacher hurrying down this road, trying to flee from God.

Many have gone "from the presence of Jehovah" by an act of disobedience. The sin of disobedience has a long and dark history. It has the distinction of being the oldest sin on record. It dates back to the time of Adam and Eve. When Satan crept into the garden on the day of the fall, he came with the most subtle temptation he had. His one aim was to separate Adam and Eve from the Lord. He wanted them to be driven "from the presence of Jehovah." He could have used any number of other temptations. He chose, however, to use his best: the temptation to disobey God's Word. It looked so innocent. Its hellishness could not be seen. It worked on that fatal day in the Garden of Eden and has worked ever since. The sin of disobedience brought the darkest day in the history of this earth, and it continues to bring dark days. One act of disobedience caused Adam and Eve the loss of everything. It left them destitute. It gave them a foretaste of hell. One act of disobedience leaves us in the same plight today. There is no temptation that should cause us to cry for help as the temptation to disobey God's Word.

All who flee "from the presence of Jehovah" come to grief and sorrow sooner or later. They take the most disappointing road a sinner can take. There is nothing but misery, confusion, darkness and regret. They finally end in hell itself—there to eternally remember the Lord's sentence—"depart from me, ye cursed, into the eternal fire which is prepared for the devil and his angels" (Matt. 25:41)—there to be eternally separated "from the presence of Jehovah."

There is hope for a repenting sinner who has fled

"from the presence of Jehovah" and calls for mercy. David found himself in this place and started to cry for mercy. Listen to him, "Cast me not away from thy presence; and take not thy holy Spirit from me. Restore unto me the joy of thy salvation; and uphold me with a willing spirit" (Ps. 51:11, 12). God honored that cry. He always does when it comes from a broken and contrite heart.

Friend, do these words perchance find you tempted to flee "from the presence of Jehovah" by some act of disobedience? Stop. Do not take another step. Don't be a Jonah. Turn and face the best Friend you have. Listen to Him ask you, "Would you also go away?" With Peter let us ask, "To whom shall we go?" With the Psalmist let us add, "Thou makest (us) glad with joy in thy presence."

7

Tarshish Ships

"He found a ship going to Tarshish" (Jonah 1:3).

If you are determined to run away from God, you will always find a ship ready to help you on your way. "Tarshish ships" are plentiful; the harbor is full of them. They leave regularly, and you never need to wait long for them. The devil himself is president of the ship company, and knows just when to have his ships ready. Jonah found that out, for he had no trouble finding "a ship going to Tarshish."

A "Tarshish ship" always sails in the opposite direction from where the Lord desires you to go. Tarshish was located west, perhaps in Spain, while Nineveh, the place to which God called Jonah, was east. The Lord leads toward the rising sun, while Satan's ships head for the setting sun. There are no ships that go to Nineveh. There is only a dusty road that leads there. It takes effort, energy and hardship to go where God calls. A Tarshish ship, however, will carry you without any effort on your part. You can even sleep as you gently glide out to sea. Is it any wonder so many would rather take a Tarshish ship than trudge the Nineveh road?

A Tarshish ship is always inviting. It is built to appeal to the eye. All of Satan's constructions are appealing. He must build so his visitors do not become suspicious. He is known as the deceiver and has perfected his art to the nth degree. He knows that the "lust of the flesh, the lust of the eye, and the vainglory of life" are his avenues of appeal. Therefore his ships are built accordingly. They are never built, however, for storms. None of his passengers ever reaches his desired destination.

Tarshish ships have various names. There is the ship *Self-will* that is steamed up to leave at a moment's notice. It has a quick get-away and is known for its speed. Then there is the ship *Good Friends* which has carried many children of God out to shipwreck. They are so surrounded by friends when this ship leaves port that they do not realize that they have left the moorings until they are out on the high seas. The ship *Pleasure* has an orchestra that plays so loudly as the ship leaves that its passengers cannot hear their friends on shore warning them. Ships —yes, no end of them—all are made and designed by the devil in his shipyards—always "going to Tarshish," never returning.

Tarshish ships glide so gently out of the harbor that you hardly realize they are going. They are the smoothest-sailing ships afloat. They never encounter a storm as they leave. They are always scheduled to sail on a sunny day in order that their passengers may be relaxed. Most of the passengers have been under a severe strain and find the sea air very conducive to sleep. The natural man is in his glory on board this ship. Sad but true, "There is a way which seemeth right unto a man; but the end thereof are the ways of death" (Prov. 14:12).

Friend, are you weary of doing God's will and desirous of a sea voyage on a Tarshish ship? Do you feel you should take a spiritual vacation? Are you tired of walking the Nineveh road and ready instead to let some ship carry you? Stop! Such suggestions are from the president of the Tarshish shipyards. Do not set foot on any of the Tarshish fleet. They are coffin ships. Even though the road that leads away from the harbor is steep, turn, call upon the Lord for help. Remember the Lord's promise, "Call upon me in the day of trouble: I will deliver thee, and thou shalt glorify me" (Ps. 50:15). Surely anyone finding himself in this harbor town is in need of crying with the Psalmist, "Make haste to help me, O Lord, my salvation" (Ps. 38:22).

8

A Mighty Tempest

"But Jehovah sent out a great wind upon the sea, and there was a mighty tempest on the sea, so that the ship was like to be broken" (Jonah 1:4).

The ship on which Jonah was a passenger sailed right into a storm. Jonah had given no thought to storms. He was so preoccupied with his own plans that it never entered his mind that he might run into violent weather. Rebellious people just do not think along that line. Satan occupies their minds with so many other thoughts that all God-inspired thoughts are sidetracked. Satan also uses his power to blind the minds of the unbelieving, that the truth should not dawn upon them (II Cor. 4:4). For this reason many lives have to be steered directly into some "mighty tempests."

Jonah had overlooked the fact that he could not get out of God's reach simply by sailing away on a Tarshish ship. The psalmist also tried to get away from God but saw he could make no headway. Finally he asked, "Whither shall I go from thy Spirit? Or whither shall I flee from thy presence?" (Psalm 139:7). He had thought of some possible hide-outs, but none could keep him away from

God. At last he gave up and cried out, "Search me, O God, and know my heart: try me, and know my thoughts; and see if there be any wicked way in me, and lead me in the way everlasting" (Psalm 139: 23, 24).

The words, "but Jehovah," which we find in this verse are the pivot point upon which Jonah's plans were turned. Many a sinner thinks his plans are perfect until he meets with a "but." The "buts" usher into the picture some unforeseen things that were not in the original plans. In Jonah's case the "but" was followed by the word "Jehovah"—"but Jehovah." The Lord was still the master of the situation. Even though He let Jonah get a running start, it took but one move on His part to catch up with Jonah. Here on the high seas He called Jonah to a halt.

The Lord's love for Jonah was not to be easily dismissed. This time His love was expressed by sending out "a great wind upon the sea." Jonah did not interpret this act as one of love. Few runaway sinners are able at first to see God's love in an act that interrupts their plans. Knowing this, God has plainly said, "My son, regard not lightly the chastening of the Lord, nor faint when thou art reproved of him; for whom the Lord loveth he chasteneth, and scourgeth every son whom he receiveth" (Heb. 12: 5, 6). We need this clear statement of the love of God in a time of chastening because Satan is then near at hand to suggest wrong interpretations. At a time of testing, it is often easier to believe the false than the true. Looking back, one saint could say about God's dealings with him, "In faithfulness thou hast afflicted me" (Ps. 119:75). He had come to recognize God's love in the affliction. That is indeed a great discovery.

The Lord has ways of causing rebellious people to think seriously. Easy sailing is often accompanied by frivolity. But somehow when "mighty tempests" blow, the atmosphere becomes conducive to sober thinking. The tossing and pitching of our frail life in a tempest seems to jar loose some really sane thinking. Many a person can testify that he turned to God in the midst of a "mighty tempest." Some of the hardest sinners have become very meek in such a setting. Many souls in heaven will continually praise God for the "mighty tempests" that they once encountered. The psalmist testified, "Before I was afflicted I went astray; but now I observe thy word" (Psalm 119:67). If it must take a "mighty tempest" to cause us to observe God's Word, then as the tempest comes let us thank God for it.

The Lord knows just how severe a tempest to send. In Jonah's case "the ship was like to be broken." The Lord could have sent a storm that would have dashed that frail ship to splinters. Had the Lord been a merciless God, the story of Jonah would no doubt have ended that way. Had the Lord not been merciful to us, our history would have been cut short years ago. Jeremiah once prayed, "O Jehovah, correct me, but in measure; not in thine anger, lest thou bring me to nothing" (Jeremiah 10:24). We would all have been brought to nothing if we had not had a loving God. All God's dealings with us are motivated by love, "for God is love" (I John 4:8). "God is faithful, who will not suffer you to be tempted above that ye are able; but will with the temptation make also the way of escape, that ye may be able to endure it" (I Cor. 10:13).

God can overtake a sinner at any place. He always meets him where he is. The particular type of tempest used to bring him to a standstill may vary with the situation, but whatever the tempest, we may be sure it is always motivated by love. This truth is beautifully summed up in the following verse: "For I know the thoughts that I think toward you, saith Jehovah, thoughts of peace, and not of evil, to give you hope in your latter end" (Jer. 29: 11). Such hope is a most precious possession. May God send what He sees fit that such a gift may be ours.

9

Asleep

"But Jonah was gone down into the innermost parts of the ship; and he lay, and was fast asleep" (Jonah 1:5).

Our friend Jonah is still going "down." He has been going down ever since he refused to obey the word of Jehovah. This time we find Jonah groping his way "down" into the dark "innermost parts of the ship." He feels he needs a nap, for he has been under quite a strain because of his conflicting thoughts. He is wise enough, however, to make his way to the "innermost parts of the ship." There is no one to bother him there, for in that part of the ship there is no activity. There he can be left alone. What a marked resemblance to a person seeking spiritual sleep! First, he is overtaken by a spirit of self-interest. Then he is not interested in watching the progress of the journey, but rather thinks only of his own comfort. Finally he withdraws from his fellowmen to find some dark "innermost" place of no activity. There is no church, however active, but some of its members become drowsy and seek places of seclusion.

Jonah no sooner finds a good resting place than

he lays himself down. There sprawled out on some improvised bed lies one of God's prophets. In this motionless position he waits for sleep to overtake him. He who was once destined to be the voice of Jehovah has chosen to lay himself down and sleep. He has decided to close his eyes to everything that is about him. It is a sad fact that many an individual who has heard the call of the Lord has thus carelessly laid himself down on some bed of ease. Friend, do you claim to be a child of God, and still find yourself inactive? Are your eyes, that were once filled with visions, getting drowsy? Then as with Jonah, you are about to fall into the worst sleep there is.

Finally Jonah "was fast asleep." He had put himself into a place where sleep was inevitable. Now he lies in a state of unconsciousness. He is absolutely helpless. He is dead to all that is around him.

There are some sober lessons that we can learn from this.

First, we notice that a sleeper is unaware of the sudden changes that are taking place. The smooth sailing vessel suddenly encounters a storm, but Jonah did not know it. He fell asleep during smooth sailing, so he was ignorant of the actual conditions around him. All sleepers are.

Secondly, a sleeper is unconcerned about his own welfare. He sees no danger, so continues to sleep on. A sleeper can be at the very verge of death, but it does not bother him. This is also true of a sleeping sinner. Hell, with all its horrors, does not stir him. He makes no effort for his own salvation while he is in this unconscious state. That is one of the reasons for much of the unconcern in our churches today.

Thirdly, a sleeper has no concern about the welfare

of his fellowmen. He can sleep on in peace while those around him are crying out in despair. Nothing bothers a sleeper. The sailors on board Jonah's ship were desperate, but it did not bother Jonah. No sleeper is concerned about others. How can he be concerned when he is unconscious?

This is a solemn lesson. It is dangerous business for a man to go wandering around in a drowsy condition. He will soon find a place to lie down, and in an unguarded moment he will be "fast asleep." For "slothfulness casteth into a deep sleep; and the idle soul shall suffer hunger" (Prov. 19:15). To all such God calls, "Awake, thou that sleepest, and arise from the dead, and Christ shall shine upon thee" (Eph. 5:14).

10

Wake Up

"So the shipmaster came to him, and said unto him, What meanest thou, O sleeper? Arise, call upon thy God, if so be that God will think upon us, that we perish not" (Jonah 1:6).

It was an exciting moment when the captain of the ship awakened Jonah by shouting above the noise of the storm, "What meanest thou, O sleeper? arise, call upon thy God." Evidently Jonah was the last one to awaken. This was no time to sleep. This was a day of trouble and a time to pray. How fitting these words are to us who are members of a church! God is calling, "Wake up." You have overslept. Time is gone that can never be regained. Awake, before you sleep away all the time of grace. The earth is ready to go to pieces. We are in a storm. Hurry—eternity is looming before us!

Notice that Jonah was nicknamed "sleeper" by the heathen captain. What a rebuke! The captain did not know that this distinguished gentleman was a prophet, so he merely chose a name that would best fit him. Oftentimes a nickname is an apt description of a person. "Sleeper"—what a descriptive nickname. It could well fit many people in our day. Friend, if some unknown person were to give you a name that would characterize you, what would it be?

Notice also, that Jonah was awakened by a group of heathen. He had purposely tried to run away from the heathen when he refused to answer God's call to go to Nineveh. When he was awakened on board ship, he found himself surrounded with nothing but heathen sailors. There is a great lesson for us in Jonah's experience. When we as Christians refuse to carry the gospel to heathen lands as we should, we also become victims of spiritual sleepiness. As we are awakened, we discover heathen around us in our very own churches. Not only are they members of our churches, but in many places they have control of the church, and are now manning it as the sailors in Jonah's day were manning the ship. If there ever was a day when the captain's words were timely, it is now. "Arise, call upon thy God, if so be that God will think upon us, that we perish not."

Then too, Jonah was urged to pray for the perishing heathen. The storm had made them desperate. They saw now that their gods were useless and therefore pleaded with Jonah to pray to his God, "if so be that God will think upon us, that we perish not." What a pathetic cry from heathen. Doesn't it grip your heart? Just think of all the heathen diligently worshipping false gods who cannot help them. We have the true God, but we are too busy sleeping to pay attention to the lost heathen. How few prayers ascend to heaven on behalf of the heathen! The prophet Samuel said, "Far be it from me that I should sin against Jehovah in ceasing to pray for you" (I Sam. 12:23). If it was a sin for Samuel to

36

neglect prayer, just think how guilty we are! Could we not by the grace of God determine today to pray for the heathen every day?

If you will tune your ear to Latin America, our closest neighbor, and listen carefully, you can hear the 125 millions crying, "What meanest thou, O sleeper? Arise, call upon thy God, if so be that God will think upon us, that we perish not." Now turn your ear to the continent of Africa, with its 150 millions. Do you not hear the same cry? Listen also to India with its 343 millions; China with its 429 millions, and then keep tuning your ear slowly to all parts of this earth, and listen to the 800 millions who have never heard the gospel. Friend, can you not hear the heathen everywhere crying the same thing, "What meanest thou, O sleeper? Arise, call upon thy God, if so be that God will think upon us, that we perish not." Is there not something you can do about it? Ah, yes. This is a day for prayer; it is no day for sleep. "The harvest indeed is plenteous, but the laborers are few. Pray ye therefore the Lord of the harvest, that he send forth laborers into his harvest" (Matt. 9:37, 38).

11

Caught

"So they cast lots, and the lot fell upon Jonah" (Jonah 1:7).

The desperate sailors resorted to casting lots in order to determine who aboard the ship might be responsible for the storm. The lot fell on Jonah! The fugitive was caught at last. Through his awakening Jonah was being shown his sinful self. Even his fellowmen knew there was something wrong with him.

The first thing that Jonah had to face after being awakened was his sin. It was sin that had mastered him like a tyrant, making him flee from Jehovah. It was sin that had fatigued him, so that he fell into a deep sleep. It was sin that had caused the mighty tempest that threatened to spell doom to himself as well as to the ship's crew. His sin had seemed so trivial at first, but now its awful consequences were only too apparent. Now he had to face it, for "the lot fell upon Jonah." A sign of a true awakening is one's attitude toward sin. The prodigal was truly awakened in the hog pen, for he determined to face his sin. "I will arise and go to my father, and will say unto him, Father, I have sinned." An awakening that does not lead to facing one's sins is useless. We are always awakened to our present condition of hopelessness in order to deal with the sins that led us there.

Jonah was learning the lesson that sin cannot be concealed. What an important lesson to learn. God's Word is very clear when it says, "Be sure your sins will find you out" (Numbers 32:23). There are those, like Jonah, who fall into sin and get away with it for some time, but then a day comes when something happens that leads to their conviction. Others again commit sin and keep it hidden from their fellowmen until their awakened conscience drives them to a confession. Still others are not caught while on this earth, but will be forced to face their sins on the judgment day. Jesus said, "For nothing is hid, that shall not be made manifest: nor anything secret, that shall not be known and come to light" (Luke 8:17). Let us not forget there is a day coming when God shall judge the secrets of men. For "there is no creature that is not manifest in his sight: but all things are naked and laid open before the eyes of him with whom we have to do" (Hebrews 4:13).

It is an act of love on God's part to let "the lot" fall on us. It shows He has not forsaken us and that His Holy Spirit has not left us, for it is His work to "convict the world in respect of sin" (John 16:8). It is far better to stand humiliated in the presence of our fellowmen than to stand some day in the presence of God and hear the words, "Depart from me, ye cursed, into the eternal fire which is prepared for the devil and his angels" (Matt. 25:41). Every time "the lot" falls on us, God is reminding us that He loves us and is calling us to repentance. Sin cannot keep us from heaven, for sin has been atoned for. Only unconfessed sin can condemn us. That is why the Lord is so gracious to let "the lot" fall on us. Then we can deal with sin, and "if we confess our sins, he is faithful and righteous to forgive us our sins, and to cleanse us from all unrighteousness" (I John 1:9).

12

Five Questions

"Tell us, we pray thee, for whose cause this evil is upon us; what is thine occupation? and whence comest thou? what is thy country? and of what people art thou? And he said unto them, I am a Hebrew; and I fear Jehovah, the God of heaven, who hath made the sea and the dry land" (Jonah 1:8, 9).

Well-aimed questions can be very embarrassing. They can expose things that are anything but pleasant, bringing to light happenings that we had hoped might be forever buried in the forgotten past. It seems that questions are always in order. We know neither who will ask them nor what will be asked next. Peter, writing to the Christians in his day, warned them as follows: "But sanctify in your hearts Christ as Lord: being ready always to give answer to every man that asketh you a reason concerning the hope that is in you, yet with meekness and fear" (I Peter 3:15). If we sanctify Christ as Lord in our hearts, many questions will no longer be embarrassing.

The five rapid questions that the inquisitive sailors asked of Jonah were very heart-searching. If Jonah had succeeded in forgetting his past up to this time, these questions forced him to face it squarely. Oftentimes God will use a pointed question asked from some unsolicited source to get a wayward sinner to stop in his tracks. Let us listen to these questions as they were asked of Jonah.

"Tell us, we pray thee, for whose cause this evil is upon us?" Jonah was faced with the fact that he had brought evil upon others. He whom God had destined to be His mouthpiece was now accused of bringing evil upon some helpless sailors. How quickly the trend of a man's life can change! In Jonah's case one act of disobedience was the pivot that turned him in the wrong direction. This question must have struck him like a blow. He who had been a champion of the cause of good was now accused of promoting evil.

Sin, regardless of its kind, is dangerous—far more so than any of us realize. It is never harvested alone by the one who sowed it. This we can easily see in the case of the first sin that was committed. Not only did Adam and Eve suffer, but the entire human race is still suffering because of it, "By the trespass of the one the many died" (Rom. 5:15). Regardless of the nature of an individual's sin, others will suffer from it either directly or indirectly. Not all, like the sailors in our text, can ask the question, "For whose cause is this evil upon us?" Perhaps it would be good for us to pause here and remind ourselves of the many who have had rough going because of our sins. Certainly it would be in place to remember all such in prayer at this time.

42

II

"What is thine occupation?" There was no way for these troubled sailors to know they were addressing a prophet. They did not have the slightest idea that they were facing an ambassador of the King of kings and Lord of lords. Up to this time Jonah had occupied his time sleeping, and no one could discern the purpose of such a life. Too many of God's representatives today are living lives like Jonah's.

It must have been a humbling experience for Jonah to look into the faces of these anxious heathen sailors and hear them ask such a question. As far as we know, this question was never asked the apostle Paul. He was never in a place very long before all who came into contact with him knew what he was there for. He himself testified, "From the *first day* that I set foot in Asia . . . I shrank not from declaring unto you anything that was profitable, and teaching you publicly, and from house to house . . . I ceased not to admonish every one night and day with tears" (Acts 20:18, 20, 31). Jesus, even at the age of twelve, testified, "I must be about my Father's business" (Luke 2:49). The early disciples lived so that the enemies of Christ "took knowledge of them, that they had been with Jesus" (Acts 4:13). Certainly all heaven-bound individuals should bear such testimony in their occupations that the lost souls around them would know their purpose in life.

III

"Whence comest thou?" In other words, "Where have you come from? Tell us about your past." This was another arresting question for Jonah to face. He had tried to run away from his past, but now he had to face it.

This question brought Jonah back to the days when he had had sweet fellowship with God. That was the place from whence he had come. God at that time had been dear to Jonah and his one great concern had been to do His will. "The word of Jehovah" had been his delight.

"Whence comest thou?" Some would have to answer: From a place where I once had simple childlike faith in Jesus Christ as Saviour, from a habit of reading the Bible daily, from a prayer closet where God was real and personal, from an active place of service in some home church, from a state of peace that passeth all understanding, from a desire to be used to win others for Christ, or, to sum it up in one statement, from a place that was a foretaste of heaven itself. Some have come a long way from this former state. They, like Jonah, merely have the sweet memories of those bygone days. Life for them has been a series of disobedient steps. But, thank God, memory can still recall those happy days of yesteryear and it does it for one purpose—to remind us that the joy of those days can still be experienced.

IV

"Where is thy country?" The sailors were concerned about Jonah's citizenship. Thus far in our study Jonah has not said a word. Had he been actively engaged in trying to win the heathen sailors for Jehovah, this question would never have been asked.

The sailors did not have the slightest idea to what King the prophet Jonah was subject. It is impossible

44

to detect a man's citizenship when he sleeps, for sleeping men bear no testimony.

No one needed to ask the apostle Paul who was his king or where he held his citizenship papers. He testified, "Our citizenship is in heaven; whence also we wait for a saviour, the Lord Jesus Christ" (Phil. 3:20). Paul lived his life as a citizen of heaven and could therefore testify, "To me to live is Christ" (Phil. 1:21). He longed for the day when he could take up his abode in the country where he held his citizenship. The direction of his life was always turned toward that country. He spent most of his time testifying about the King of kings—Jesus Christ his Saviour.

If someone were to ask you, "Where is thy country?" how would you answer? Can people tell by observing you that you are a citizen of heaven? Is there anything about you that indicates you are waiting for the Saviour——"the Lord Jesus Christ"?

"Of what people art thou?" In other words, who are your friends? You can often judge a person by the company he keeps, for "birds of a feather will flock together." The sailors, knowing this truth, felt that an answer to this question would throw light upon the serious situation in which they found themselves.

If a person is left to himself, he will always find his way to people of a similar spirit. We read of the apostles, "And being let go, they came to their own company" (Acts 4:23). When the restraints of home are lifted, a prodigal will soon be surrounded by companions of a like spirit. A Christian, on the other hand, will find friends who love the Saviour. A good check of our whereabouts is a check on our associates.

"Of what people art thou?" Paul wrote that the Ephesians were "fellow-citizens with the saints, and of the household of God" (Eph. 2:19). They belonged to the best of people. Most people belong to the other group, outside the family of God, a people that will some day hear the sentence pronounced upon them, "Depart from me, ye cursed, into the eternal fire which is prepared for the devil and his angels" (Matt. 25:41). To which of these two groups do you belong?

Five sobering questions awaited an answer. Jonah answered the last question first by saying, "I am a Hebrew" (v. 9). By this answer, he introduced himself as a member of the family of God's people.

He summed up the answer to the other questions by saying, "I fear Jehovah, the God of heaven, who hath made the sea and the dry land" (v. 9). He still feared Jehovah, even if he had disobeyed Him. Many sinners who are bent on going their own way still retain the fear of the Lord in their hearts. Somehow neither Tarshish ships nor any other kind of ship can sail far enough to get away from the fear of God. Praise God, dear friend, if this holy fear is still your possession. Remember, "The fear of Jehovah is the beginning of wisdom; and the knowledge of the Holy One is understanding" (Prov. 9:10). There is still hope for all who still have the fear of Jehovah in their hearts.

13

A Question That Only You Can Answer

"What is this that thou hast done?" (Jonah 1:10).

Another question that the terrified sailors asked Jonah was, "What is this that thou hast done?" It was much the same as the piercing question, "What hast thou done?"that God asked guilty Cain many years before. Let us also face this question squarely and allow God's Word to pry into our hearts.

First, "What is this that thou hast done?" Have you wasted your life? Are you today what years ago you thought you would be? Have the visions that God gave you on the mount of inspiration been fulfilled? Or have you lived your life for your own fleshly satisfaction? Jonah took a ship to a far port to escape his God-appointed duty. Have you perhaps sought to evade God's call by an excursion into worldly pleasure? Have you let your life drift into some terrible storm? Answer truthfully, what is this that you have done with your life?

Secondly, let us change the question to read, "What is this that thou hast NOT done?" In Jonah's case it was not so much what he had done as what he had neglected to do. He had failed to bring the word of God to the heathen. He was guilty of the sin of omission. It will be because of similar sins of omission that Jesus will condemn some of the nations of the world when He returns in glory. He will tell them, "Depart from me, ye cursed, into the eternal fire which is prepared for the devil and his angels: for I was hungry, and ye did not give me to eat; I was thirsty, and ye gave me no drink; I was a stranger, and ye took me not in; naked, and ye clothed me not; sick, and in prison, and ye visited me not . . . Inasmuch as ye did it not unto one of these least, ye did it not unto me" (Matt. 25:41-45). Notice, they are not cast out because of evil works done, but because of good works not done. What a solemn warning to us! Think of the many souls that could have been saved if we had been fully yielded to our Lord! Think how greatly God's power could have been manifested to this worldly generation, if we had remained closer to our Saviour! Think how many perishing tribes and peoples could now have the gospel if we had been men of faith like William Carey, David Livingstone, Hudson Taylor, and others. Yes, think, and let the question convict our hearts: "What is this that thou hast NOT DONE?"

Now, let us change the question once more, "What is this that thou canst YET DO?" Praise God, dear friend, we are still in the day of grace. There is yet time for something to be done. God is still able to change failures to successes and make us into His good and faithful servants.

If this is true, then what should we do? First, let us admit our sins. Let us take time right now to talk to the Lord, for He is not far from any of us. By His grace let us cling to the promise, "I, even I, am he that blotteth out thy transgression for mine own sake; and I will not remember thy sins" (Isa. 43:25). Secondly, let us turn the rest of our lives over to Him. Our journey's end may be near, but we still can yield. Our God is so mighty that He will do as He has promised, "I will restore to you the years that the locust hath eaten" (Joel 2:25). He can give us a bumper blessing in the days to come. By the daily strength that He will provide, He will enable us to say, "Not my will, but thine be done."

"What is this that thou hast done?" How pleasing this same question now sounds! It offers us an opportunity to testify: "I bring my sins to Christ and He accepts me. I turn my life over to Him that He may be my Master and King."

14

What Shall We Do?

"What shall we do unto thee that the sea may be calm unto us?" (Jonah 1:11).

These frantic words were shouted into the ears of Jonah above the noise of the storm. The sailors had become desperate. They thought that at any moment they would be plunged into a watery grave. The howling wind, the angry waves, and the frail ship together created an atmosphere of helplessness and despair.

The sailors' question was personal. Previously they had been concerned about Jonah; now they were concerned about themselves. The intensity of the storm had brought them to the breaking point— their one concern was to be saved. "What shall WE do?" Praise God for any "mighty tempest" that will show us our helplessness and make us concerned about our eternal welfare. There is hope for all who find themselves in such a situation.

This question came from men in despair. It takes a mighty tempest from Jehovah to bring us to this place. Other storms can be outridden by casting forth "the wares that are in the ship" (v. 5) but not this storm. Our own wisdom and skill, which in the past have proved such efficient pilots, are now useless. This storm is different. "Jehovah had sent out a great wind upon the sea and there was a mighty tempest" (v. 4). No human being can weather such a storm. It only becomes "more and more tempestuous" (v. 13). It is like God's holy law. No one can survive in its presence. It will toss us about until it drives us to despair, for "there is none righteous, no, not one" (Rom. 3:10). Its purpose is to rage until it has brought us to the place where we shall cry out, "What shall we do?" The sooner it brings us to this place, the sooner we will find deliverance.

The question of the sailors is not an uncommon one. It is a question that has led to great deliverances. On the day of Pentecost, Peter's sermon plunged thousands of souls into a mighty tempest. In their agony of heart, they cried out, "Brethren, what shall we do?" Let us now listen to the exact answer that Peter gave: "Repent ye, and be baptized every one of you in the name of Jesus Christ unto the remission of your sins: and ye shall receive the gift of the Holy Spirit. For to you is the promise, and to your children, and to all that are afar off, even as many as the Lord our God shall call unto him" (Acts 2:37-39). Three thousand people, responding to this answer, received deliverance. The Philippian jailer, when an earthquake released his prisoners, also found himself in the worst tempest he had ever faced. It drove him to his knees, where he cried out, "What must I do to be saved?" Listen carefully, friend, to Paul's answer. It may be the one you have been waiting for: "Believe on the Lord Jesus, and thou shalt be saved, thou and thy house" (Acts 16:30, 31). The jailer's mighty tempest ceased immediately. This man, who a few minutes before had been on the verge of committing suicide, was gloriously saved.

Does this day find you in a storm? Has a siege of restlessness gripped you? Are you tossed about until you are ready to give up? Are you high up on some crest one day and the next down in despair? Are you bewildered and driven far from the course you started on? Are the storm clouds hanging low so you see no horizons? Does the cry come from your soul, "What shall I do?" Then let me point you now to Jesus Christ the Saviour. He is "a very present help in trouble" (Ps. 46:1). He is the answer to this question, as well as to all other questions. Let us cry out with the disciples, "Save, Lord; we perish." Note the result of that short, simple prayer: "He arose, and rebuked the winds and the sea; and there was a great calm" (Matt. 8:25, 26).

15

How to Deal With Sin

"Take me up, and cast me forth into the sea; so shall the sea be calm unto you: for I know that for my sake this great tempest is upon you" (Jonah 1: 12).

The above words were Jonah's answer to the sailors' question, "What shall we do?" If they were to have a calm sea, it was up to them to make the next move. No doubt this answer shocked them, for it had not dawned upon them that they would have to pay such a price.

"Take me up," said Jonah—up out of the innermost parts of the ship to the open deck above. God's answer to a troubled sinner is similar. He pleads that all sin that has hidden itself down in the innermost recesses of our hearts be brought to light. Sometimes the cause of our trouble can lie undetected for years, but when once it is found, it is up to us to bring it into the open. The Lord's word is still good —"Only acknowledge thine iniquity, that thou hast transgressed against Jehovah thy God. . . . Return, ye backsliding children, I will heal your backslidings" (Jer. 3:13, 22).

To confess sin is about as difficult a task as we

ever attempt. Our very nature rebels. If we never realized before that we were proud, we can easily see it when we contemplate exposing the inner closets of our wicked hearts. However, we cannot hide anything from our God, for He "knoweth the secrets of the heart" (Ps. 44:21), and "there is nothing . . . hid, that shall not be known" (Matt. 10:26). That being the case, it is far better that we ourselves "take up" anything in our past lives that needs to be dealt with than to wait and have it all exposed at the judgment seat.

"Cast me forth," continues Jonah. In other words, separate yourselves from me. CAST is a strong word. When we cast something, we usually do so not expecting to pick it up again. We are admonished in God's Word, "Cast thy burden upon Jehovah, and he will sustain thee" (Ps. 55:22). Here, also, the word Cast is used to admonish us to be forever through with our burden. King Hezekiah once testified in prayer, "Thou hast CAST all my sins behind thy back" (Isa. 38:17). The Lord had cast them there because he was through with them forever. Jonah, knowing he was the cause of the trouble, advised the sailors to cast him forth.

Simply to take up a sin and then refuse to cast it forth does no good. That is like digging out half a sliver which has imbedded itself in your finger, leaving the other half to fester. Many people are in the state of always confessing a sin but never getting to the place of victory over it. That is mocking God. There must be both a taking-up and a cast-forth. This truth is brought out very clearly in the verse, "He that covereth his transgressions shall not prosper; but whoso confesseth [takes up] and forsaketh [casts forth] them shall obtain mercy" (Prov. 28:13).

Jonah further states, "For I know that for my sake this great tempest is upon you." Many a sinner "knows" much more than he will admit. If every sinner would confess all that he knows, his problems would be quickly solved. How foolish to know, yet do nothing about it. Some frank sinners admit that they have known all the time what their sins were. The Holy Spirit, whose work it is to convict of sin, has been working in their hearts. There is no hope for a sinner whom the Holy Spirit cannot convict of sin. Such individuals have not come the first step toward being saved. Therefore, when we know what is wrong with us, let us admit with David, "I know my transgressions; and my sin is ever before me" (Ps. 51:3).

"For my sake this tempest is upon you," Jonah admitted. This truth must have caused deep anguish in Jonah's soul. It is hard to see others suffer, but it becomes torture to see them suffer when we know we have been the cause of it. In many instances the suffering of the one who is the cause of the trouble, multplies a hundredfold. A speeding driver refused his wife's advice to slow down. His car skidded into the ditch and overturned. His wife was killed. Overcome with grief, he refused to be comforted, crying, "It was all my fault!"

All tempests have a cause. Many a person's gray hairs, if they could speak, would tell a revealing story. Premature funerals have often been held for causes other than those announced in the obituaries. Many a tear, if it could reveal its source, would expose a pathetic story. Most of the time we see but the effect of trouble, and seldom trace it back to its source.

Have you ever tried to list all the tempests of which you have been the cause? Many tempests are started by a lie, an unkind word, an act of selfishness, misunderstanding, pride, jealousy, stubbornness, thoughtlessness, lack of love or the like. If we were to be honest, we would have to confess with Jonah, "For my sake this tempest is upon you." Do you think there are any tempests raging now in someone's heart because of you? Do not lie down to rest this night until you have done something about it. Pray for strength to be as honest and frank as Jonah.

16

Trying Hard?

"Nevertheless the men rowed hard to get them back to the land; but they could not: for the sea grew more and more tempestuous against them" (Jonah 1:13).

This scene reminds one of a lost sinner who is drifting on the sea of life. He realizes his danger and tries his utmost to reach safety. At times he thinks he is making headway, and then another gigantic wave tosses him farther back than ever. His best efforts avail him nothing, leaving him only exhausted with his last hope of salvation gone.

The best these sailors could do was not enough to save them. They strained every muscle when they "rowed hard to get them back to land." It was a life and death struggle. If there had been any salvation for them in hard work, these men would have found it. However, the harder they rowed, the worse the storm raged. Their best efforts brought them no place, but left them utterly exhausted. What a lesson for a struggling soul who is trying to have himself by doing the best he can! Martin Luther tried for years to save himself. He worked so desperately at it that he nearly lost his health as well as his soul.

Saving oneself is utterly impossible. To "do the best you can" sounds nice to be sure, but it is contrary to God's way of salvation.

It was never God's plan that the sailors on Jonah's ship should get out of this tempest by their "hard rowing." It was His plan to let the sea grow more and more tempestuous against them until they gave up in despair. Neither is it God's plan that any soul should save himself by his own good works. If we try that, we are making the wrong use of God's law. "We know that the law is good, if a man use it lawfully" (I Tim. 1:8). To try to ease a stormy conscience by our good works is a waste of time. It is worse than that. It places us under a curse! "As many as are of the works of the law are under a curse" (Gal. 3:10). Such works take up our time and energy and give us a false hope. The Lord's plan of salvation is just the opposite from that of works. Listen to Him again, as He speaks, "For by grace have ye been saved through faith; and that not of yourselves, it is the gift of God: not of works, that no man should glory" (Eph. 2:8, 9). It is God's plan that not one ounce of work on our part (hard rowing) is to be added to His plan of salvation. If it is added, there is no salvation.

There are many distressed souls who are still exhausting themselves at the oars. Religious? Yes. Sincere? Definitely! Trying hard? Desperately, but to no avail. Who are such people? They are all those who base their salvation on their own good works. For example, there are those people who think they are saved because they go to church or they contribute to some worthy cause. Still others base their salvation on the fact that they pray, or they read the Bible, or they live good clean moral lives. Such people are in the position of Israel of old who "followed after a law of righteousness," but did not arrive at the law. "Wherefore? Because they sought it not by faith, but, as it were, by works [hard rowing]" (Rom. 9:31, 32). But the Gentiles, on the other hand, "who followed not after righteousness [quit rowing], attained to righteousness, even the righteousness which is of faith" (Rom. 9:30).

God would, through this text, call a stop to all who are trying to save themselves by their own struggling. To have good intentions, to change one's ways, to make resolutions and to try hard—all sound good to the natural man, but they avail nothing. These are vain attempts at the oars of human ability to bring us to salvation. We are doomed with this method for the sea only becomes "more and more tempestuous." It is time to stop struggling in our own strength and call to Jesus Christ, our Saviour, to take over.

Ask Him who "came to seek and to save that which was lost" (Luke 19:10) to take over your case. Away with the oars! Let us accept God's way out of this tempest. "Being therefore justified *by faith* we have peace with God through our Lord Jesus Christ" (Rom. 5:1).

17

Facing Death

*"We beseech thee, O Jehovah, we beseech thee,
let us not perish for this man's life, and lay not upon
us innocent blood; for thou, O Jehovah, hast done
as it pleased thee"* (Jonah 1:14).

Many people face death by praying. There is no
better way. The above Scripture was the prayer of
the terrified sailors who were already in the clutches
of death. The most solemn moment of their lives
had come. All their efforts to outride the storms had
resulted in failure. They had prayed "every man
unto his own god"; they had tried sacrificing by
casting forth the wares that were in the ship; they
had rowed hard to get back to land, but all this had
failed. At least when all hope was gone, they cast
themselves on the mercy of the living God. The
"mighty tempest" had produced its desired effects.
May no tempest subside until it brings us to this
place!

Listen to these men pray. Recorded here is one of
the most sincere prayer meetings ever held. There
was not a drowsy moment, not a wandering thought.
All these men meant what they said. They knew
what they wanted and lost no time putting it into

words. Then, too, the storm had brought them to a place where they were all in the same position. They could use the pronoun WE, instead of crying "every man unto his own god." There was no spirit of criticism or fault-finding among them. Death was staring them in the face; they knew they were lost and must act quickly. All who find themselves in such a situation can really pray.

This was a prayer of utter dependence upon Jehovah. For the first time on board this ship prayer was offered to Jehovah. Until this moment these sailors had not needed Him. Now they must have Him. Many people leave Jehovah out of their lives until they are facing death; then suddenly they become sober. Their past comes rushing by in a moment's time. Sins that have been forgotten for years come back to the memory as if they had just happened. It is then that they see the folly of sin. How they regret that Jehovah has been ignored! How many times these words have been repeated—"Oh, if only I could live my life over again!"

This prayer was a cry for salvation. "Let us not perish." What well-chosen words! These men who just a few moments before had been rank heathen, had already learned to pray. After all the greatest school of prayer is the school of need. Let an individual fully realize he is about to be plunged into an eternal death, and you will hear him cry for salvation with all his heart. There is no need of priming such a one to pray. In fact, you cannot prevent him from praying. The hardest sinner will then melt. Our Saviour is waiting for sinners to pray for salvation. Dear friend, do you sense your need of salvation, for yourself as well as for your family? Feel free to use this same prayer; it has no copyrights attached to it. It brought salvation once and can bring it again. Simply cry with the sailors of old, "O Jehovah, we beseech thee, let us not perish."

This prayer was also a cry of submission. "For thou, O Jehovah, hast done as it pleased thee." The sailors were not finding fault with Jehovah but were simply yielding to Him. Like clay in the hands of the potter, they had become meek and pliable. This was their way of saying, "Not my will, but thine be done." All who come to this place in prayer are soon ready for a great deliverance. This indeed is real praying. We are not to pray to make Jehovah submissive to us, but rather that He will make us submissive to Him.

How wonderful that we have a God who will hear us when we cry in such dire moments of need. Even though we have been busy serving the gods of this world, still Jehovah is merciful to hear when we call upon Him. The hour of death, however, is a poor time to call for salvation. Often the pain is too severe to allow sober thinking. Medicine is often given that dulls the senses and puts the patient in a stupor. Then, too, death may come unannounced and give no time for even the shortest prayer. Let us, therefore, pray NOW the prayer of the sailors, "O Jehovah, we beseech thee, let us not perish."

18

Prayer Brings Results

"So they took up Jonah, and cast him forth into the sea; and the sea ceased from its raging" (Jonah 1:15).

The sailors have another lesson of paramount importance to teach us. In the previous verse we witnessed their prayer service. In this text we see the result of that prayer. It is always interesting to see what happens after people pray.

First we notice that prayer led to obedience. The sailors were no sooner through praying than they pitched Jonah overboard. True prayer always leads to obedience. Scripture has many examples of this truth. The ten lepers did well when they cried out to Jesus, "Master, have mercy on us" (Luke 17:13). This prayer, however, would have been useless had they not obeyed the Lord when He said, "Go and show yourselves unto the priests." As they obeyed, they received their blessing, for we read, "As they went, they were cleansed" (v. 14).

Prayer and obedience go hand in hand. One can never be substituted for the other. It is far better to cut our prayer short as the sailors did, and act in obedience to what we know to be the will of God, than to think we "shall be heard for [our] much speaking" (Matt. 6:7). No one has yet talked himself around God. One act of obedience is worth more than a thousand prayers that are a substitute for obedience. When prayer becomes a means of simply easing our conscience and becomes a substitute for obedience, it is useless. There are too many people who use prayer in this way. Year after year goes by and they still refuse to act in obedience to what they know to be God's will. To such prayer, God says, "I will hide my eyes from you; yea, when you make many prayers, I will not hear" (Isa. 1:15). "Obedience is better than sacrifice," cried the prophet to King Saul who was trying to hide his disobedience behind worship. Obedience has no substitute. Christ is "unto all them that OBEY him the author of eternal salvation" (Heb. 5:9).

The sailors were willing to separate themselves from the cause of their trouble. "They took up Jonah, and cast him forth into the sea." Since Jonah was the cause of their trouble, they had to deal with him. This was not easy to do. In fact, they had tried everything they could think of to avoid this very act. How hard it is for us human beings to deal with the cause of our trouble. We will often keep sins hidden away in our hearts for years rather than part with them. We will lengthen our prayers, increase our good works, make many sacrifices, if only we can be spared from this act. It is only as a last resort, when we see that all hope is gone, that we are willing to confess and part with sin.

Sin never leaves of its own accord. Like Jonah, it will cling to us through the worst storms. Jonah, the cause of the sailors' trouble, did not jump into the sea himself; the sailors "took up Jonah, and cast him forth into the sea." It took a definite act on their part. He was to go into the sea to be forever separated from them.

Our God also has a sea into which He has promised to sink our sins. "He will again have compassion upon us; he will tread our iniquities under foot; and thou wilt cast all their sins into the depths of the sea" (Micah 7:19). Praise God there is a "sea" that stands ready to receive the sins that are causing us our troubles. Let us say with the Psalmist, "I will confess my transgressions unto Jehovah" (Ps. 32:5).

The sailors found out that a troubled sea can be calmed. "The sea ceased from its raging." They learned, however, that they could not keep the cause of their troubles and experience calmness at the same time. This lesson was hard to learn. Now that they had actually experienced it, they saw the folly of their past labors. How foolish to have retained Jonah so long! Even if he was the most precious part of their cargo, it was a mistake to keep him. Now they saw it clearly. They had learned a secret. The formula is in our text: "Took up . . . cast forth." Take up the cause of your troubles. Hold it forth before the Lord. Regardless of how it may squirm and twist, hold it firmly in simple confession. Then drop it once and for all! Remember the promise: "If we confess our sins he is faithful and righteous to forgive us our sins and cleanse us from all unrighteousness" (I John 1:9). This is God's way of quieting a storm. It worked in the life of the sailors, and it works today. By God's grace, let us throw overboard all the sins that cause us our troubles today. With the song writer let us say:

> *"The dearest idol I have known,*
>   *Whate'er that idol be,*
> *Help me to tear it from Thy throne,*
>   *And worship only Thee."*

Then we, too, can testify that our God "stilleth the roaring of the seas, the roaring of their waves" (Ps. 65:7).

19

Honoring Jehovah

"Then the men feared Jehovah exceedingly; and they offered a sacrifice unto Jehovah, and made vows" (Jonah 1:16).

We are about to bid farewell to the sailors. Since we started our journey with Jonah, these men have taught us many lessons. They have one more lesson to teach us before they leave. There were three things that they did immediately after the storm subsided that are worth observing.

First, they "feared Jehovah exceedingly." It is always interesting to notice what happens to an individual after the Lord has answered his prayer. In the case of the nine lepers, they forgot to return to give God glory. What a common mistake! If ever there is an easy time to forget the Lord, it is after He has answered our request. The sailors, however, did not fall into this error. Their deliverance had been so great that a holy respect called "fear" had gripped them. Their own unworthiness in comparison to Jehovah's greatness had produced an exceeding great "fear." This is as it should be, for we are told to "serve Jehovah with fear" (Ps. 2:11). "The fear of Jehovah is the beginning of wisdom" (Prov.

9:10), and "the fear of Jehovah is a fountain of life" (Prov. 14:27)

Secondly, "they offered a sacrifice." Whatever it was that they had aboard the ship to use as a sacrifice, it met with Jehovah's approval. And that is the most important thing about a sacrifice—that God accepts it. But, the question arises, does God expect sacrifices in our day? Indeed He does. His Word is very clear on this point. Wherever an individual may find himself, he too, like the sailors in our text, can offer a sacrifice. There are at least five different sacrifices that can be made even if one's earthly means are as limited as those of the sailors.

1. The first is a BROKEN AND A CONTRITE SPIRIT. "The sacrifices of God are a broken spirit: a broken and a contrite heart, O God, thou wilt not despise" (Ps. 51:17).

2. The second is JOY. The Psalmist affirmed, "I will offer in his tabernacle sacrifices of joy" (Ps. 27:6).

3. The third is PRAISE. "Through him [Christ] then let us offer up a sacrifice of praise to God continually, that is, the fruit of lips which make confession to his name" (Heb. 13:15).

4. The fourth is THANKSGIVING. "Offer unto God the sacrifice of thanksgiving" (Ps. 50:14). "Whoso offereth the sacrifice of thanksgiving glorifieth me" (Ps. 50:23)

5. The fifth is OURSELVES. "Present your bodies a living sacrifice, holy, acceptable to God, which is your spiritual service" (Rom. 12:1).

These are but five of the sacrifices that are well-pleasing to Jehovah. Are they familiar to you?

Thirdly, the sailors "made vows." They were so

impressed with Jehovah's great salvation that they determined right then and there to bind themselves to Him in some way. This they did when they made vows. When once a young man has found the girl who makes him happy, he is eager for the day when he can make vows to take her as his wife. Then she will be his for all time. When once an individual has met Christ, who can satisfy the longing of the heart, he, too, will joyfully and spontaneously make a vow. This vow unites him to Christ in a spiritual wedding. It is made to be kept forever. For "when a man voweth a vow unto Jehovah, or sweareth an oath to bind his soul with a bond, he shall not break his word; he shall do according to all that proceedeth out of his mouth" (Num. 30:2). However, as vows made between human beings are not always kept, so also vows made to God are broken. This is an abomination. We are warned, "When thou vowest a vow unto God, defer not to pay it; for he hath no pleasure in fools: pay that which thou vowest. Better is it that thou shouldest not vow, than that thou shouldest vow and not pay" (Ecc. 5:4, 5). Oh, for grace to be as the Psalmist who said, "So will I sing praise unto thy name for ever, that I may daily perform my vows" (Ps. 61:8).

When once a vow has been made to God, it is binding. Jacob made a vow the time he fled from home. Evidently he had forgotten about it, but after twenty years the Lord appeared to him and said, "I am the God of Bethel, where thou anointedst a pillar, where thou vowedst a vow unto me: now arise, get thee out from this land, and return unto the land of thy nativity" (Gen. 31:13). O friend, you who once stopped at a Bethel, can you not hear your loving Lord reminding you today to keep that vow? He has been faithful on His part. He is like a faithful mate who has been deserted, but still waits for you to return. The vow still stands. By God's grace, let us determine "I will pay my vows unto Jehovah" (Ps. 116:14).

20

"A Great Fish"

"And Jehovah prepared a great fish to swallow up Jonah" (Jonah 1:17a).

Many people see only the fish in this verse and fail to see Jehovah who made it. This accounts for so much of the doubt and ridicule held by many in connection with this part of the Book of Jonah. There is no inspiration in a slippery fish apart from the Lord who prepared it. Unless we see that this experience of Jonah was a type of salvation, we will miss the blessings of this book.

The fish was God's plan of salvation: it was He who prepared it. There was no suggestion from Jonah or the sailors as to how salvation might come. The situation looked hopeless to them. It never even dawned upon them that Jehovah had a plan of salvation for such a disobedient man as Jonah. But our God is Love. He planned salvation for Jonah; He planned and prepared a way of salvation for us too. This He did even before He created the world. "He chose us in him before the foundation of the world" (Eph. 1:4). His plan was fully carried out in Christ, and was finished on Calvary.

There was nothing in Jonah that merited salvation. He had deliberately disobeyed the Lord. His sin had caused grief and suffering to those that were associated with him, as well as to himself. Now when he found himself sinking in a sea of despair, God had "prepared" a way of salvation for him. What a merciful God! He gives salvation to those who do not merit it—in fact, *only* to those. His word says: "For by grace have ye been saved through faith: and that not of yourselves, it is the gift of God; not of works, that no man should glory" (Eph. 2:8, 9).

The "prepared" fish was Jonah's only way of salvation. The Lord never has two ways of salvation. When mankind was to be saved from the flood, there was only one ark prepared for them. When God fellowshipped with Israel in the wilderness, there was only one tabernacle. Only one temple was built in the land of promise. When in the fulness of time God sent forth His Son to be the Saviour of this world, He came alone. There was no other salvation. Jesus said, "I am the way, and the truth, and the life; no one cometh unto the Father, but by me" (John 14:6). "In none other is there salvation: for neither is there any other name under heaven, that is given among men, wherein we must be saved" (Acts 4:12).

When Jonah entered this God-planned way of salvation, as he was swallowed by the great fish, it seemed to the onlookers to be the end of him. So also think the friends of this world when they witness one of their companions entering into the life of salvation. Paul's companions became so irritated at him when he became a Christian that they even made plans to kill him. To the onlooker who does not understand the way of salvation it does look hopeless. For "the word of the cross is to them that perish foolishness: but unto us who are saved, it is the power of God" (I Cor. 1:18).

Jehovah went to a lot of bother to save one man. He always values an individual very highly and no expense is too great to save one soul. We do not know how many years the fish was in the preparatory stage before it was called upon to perform this mission. It is enough for us to know that this act of Jehovah's revealed His infinite love for a disobedient man. Jehovah is indeed longsuffering "not wishing that any should perish but that all should come to repentance" (II Peter 3:9).

God so loved Jonah that He prepared a great fish; but "God so loved the world that He gave His only begotten Son that whosoever believeth on Him should not perish but have eternal life" (John 3:16).

21

God's School Room

"And Jonah was in the belly of the fish three days and three nights" (Jonah 1:17b).

The belly of the fish, which at first seemed to be the place of Jonah's doom, turned out to be God's prepared school room for him. What a slimy unattractive place it was. There was no ventilation or light. Slime and blackness enfolded him. There was not a single friend to whom he could turn. It was in this place of utter seclusion with no door of escape that God chose to teach Jonah some lessons he would never forget.

God's school room can be any place. He is not fussy about the place just so it is one where He can get the undivided attention of His pupil. Oftentimes it is the sick room. Great lessons have been learned here. It seems that some of us can learn better when we are stretched out in a horizontal position. Our upward look is easier in this position than in any other. Sometimes the lesson seems prolonged, and we become impatient and seek dismissal. However, no pupil is dismissed until the lesson is learned, and the teacher Himself announces that the class is over. Some pupils have been so completely changed in this class room of sickness that they have become happy and content to stay on there with their beloved Teacher until called home by death.

For others the school room may be a place of misfortune or disappointment. The prodigal son found himself in just such a place. He did not get into a teachable spirit until he "spent all" and "began to be in want" (Luke 15:14). It was there that "he came to himself" and confessed, "Father, I have sinned." After being taught this lesson, he could be dismissed to put into practice what he had learned. Many people are not approachable by God until everything has been taken away from them. God had to wait until Jacob was alone and friendless before He could reveal to him the ladder that reached to heaven. It was in that helpless, empty position, overwhelmed by loneliness, that Jacob said, "Surely Jehovah is in this place; and I knew it not. . . . This is none other than the house of God and this is the gate of heaven" (Gen. 28:16, 17). It is this type of school room that has been the turning point in the lives of many.

They who find themselves in God's school room are absolutely helpless, being weighed down with great concern. All giggling, jesting and foolishness are quickly dismissed. Those who submit to God's will sense His nearness and receive a great blessing. Many a pupil has been gloriously blessed when he has laid claim to the promise, "God is our refuge and strength, a very present help in trouble" (Ps. 46:1).

Satan hates God's school room and is a frequent visitor there. He is determined to hinder all from receiving the blessings that God is ready to impart.

He therefore injects thoughts of rebellion into the hearts of the pupils. As a result, some of the pupils are tempted to complain because they have been taken aside from their usual walk of life. Others have been tempted to believe that God does not care for them. To these and to all others thus tempted, God would still their fears with the promise, "I know the thoughts that I think toward you, saith Jehovah, thoughts of peace, and not of evil, to give you hope in your latter end" (Jer. 29:11).

The chapter ends with mercy—God providing a means of salvation for an unworthy man. In fact, all four chapters of this book close with a presentation of God's mercy. How wonderful to know that He is merciful! "Jehovah, a God merciful and gracious, slow to anger and abundant in loving kindness and truth" (Ex. 34:6). Note that "merciful" leads the list. Our God has a mercy seat. Oh pupils of His school room, "Let us therefore draw near with boldness unto the throne of grace, that we may receive mercy and may find grace to help us in time of need" (Heb. 4:16).

22

A Plea in Distress

"Then Jonah prayed unto Jehovah his God out of the fish's belly" (Jonah 2:1).

"Then Jonah prayed." We waited for this all through chapter one. In almost every verse, Jonah had occasion to pray, but not once did we find him on his knees. We saw him sitting, running, sleeping and talking, but never praying. Now it is different, for chapter two begins with the word "then." "Then Jonah prayed."

There never was a period in Jonah's life when he prayed as he did at this particular time. He was not just reciting some well worn prayer sentences, but he was actually praying. The circumstances in which he found himself left only one avenue of escape—prayer. Jonah therefore opened his heart to God and cried out in real earnestness. Is that the way you pray? Have you by chance fallen into the rut of merely uttering mechanical prayers? Our Saviour, knowing our weakness on this point, warned us, "In praying use not vain repetitions as the Gentiles do: for they think that they shall be heard for their much speaking" (Matt. 6:7). Prayer is not mental gymnastics; it is opening one's heart to God.

It is only when we pray in such a manner that we can expect results. If you sense a lack of depth and power in your prayer life, turn to Christ and ask as the disciples did years ago, "Lord teach us to pray" (Luke 11:1)

Our careless praying must grieve God. In one instance He said, "Ye have not because ye ask not" (James 4:2). Think of all we could have from God today if we would only take time to pray. Again God has said, "Ye ask, and receive not, because ye ask amiss, that ye may spend it in your pleasures" (James 4:3). How selfish many of our prayers must sound in God's ears.

The importance of prayer is emphasized all through the Bible. The people through whom God has worked have been men and women of prayer. Their successes or failures can be traced to their prayer habits. God has seen fit to limit the advancement of His great program of salvation to the prayers of His people. Therefore He has said, "If my people, who are called by my name, will humble themselves and *pray*, and seek my face, and turn from their wicked ways: *then* will I hear from heaven, and will forgive their sins, and will heal their land" (II Chron. 7:14).

God has made it possible for anyone to be saved who will pray. The promise reads, "Whosoever shall *call* upon the name of the Lord shall be saved" (Rom. 10:13). How simple and emphatic this verse is. God takes it for granted that anybody can call. He therefore has placed salvation within the reach of all of us.

Deliverance of all kinds is conditioned by prayer. The Lord has said, "Call unto me: and I will answer thee, and will show thee great things and difficult which thou knowest not" (Jer. 33:3). If we, like Jonah, neglect to call unto the Lord, we shall be left to our own doom; on the other hand if we call unto Him, the promise is ours. Prayer therefore becomes the pivot upon which the events of our life are turned.

Many people are fast heading for destruction because they neglect prayer. This was Jonah's mistake. However, when he started to pray, the events of his life began to change. Everyone can pray if he wants to; for, although prayer requires the grace of God, it is a grace that He gives freely to all who ask for it. The reason we fail to pray is not that we *cannot* pray but that we do not *care* to pray. Prayerlessness can often be traced to laziness for the two are closely related.

Praise God for anything that leads us into a prayer life, even if it be trials of various kinds. Those who never had time for prayer before, suddenly find themselves praying in times of great need. It was that way with Jonah, "*THEN* Jonah prayed." Even those who ridicule Christ and prayer in the days of their prosperity will pray in times of dire need. Paul did. When he became blinded so that he had to be "led by the hand," we read the report, "Behold, he prayeth" (Acts 9:11). It took a mighty blow from God to bring this man to his knees. Backsliders, too, find their way back to their neglected prayer closets in a hurry when trouble comes.

Some wait to pray until it is too late. The rich man in Hades prayed a wonderful prayer when he cried, "Have mercy on me" (Luke 16:24). Nothing was wrong with the prayer. It was a perfect prayer, and one that had brought great results to many others. The only thing wrong was that he waited until it was too late. How tragic! No matter where these lines may find you—pray. Pray now. "Pray without ceasing" (I Thess. 5:17). Jesus said, "For men ought always to PRAY and not to faint" (Luke 18:1).

23

Affliction

"I called by reason of mine affliction unto Jehovah. . . . Out of the belly of Sheol cried I" (Jonah 2:1).

This is the first of seven statements with the pronoun "I" which Jonah made while entombed within the fish. We shall note with interest what Jonah now has to say about himself in this strange schoolroom in which Jehovah has placed him. There are two "I's" in this first verse, but since they are so closely related we shall deal with them as one.

These words of our text constitute lesson number one that Jonah learned in this strange place. This first lesson teaches a great truth: that affliction, if taken in the right way, can lead to great blessings. This is not an easy lesson to learn. Some have struggled with it for years before they have seen its truth and relaxed. Jonah was already in the clutches of death before he learned it.

Affliction can be a means of driving us to the Lord. Jehovah said of the people in Hosea's day, "I will go and return to my place, till they acknowledge their offence, and seek my face: in their *affliction* they will seek me earnestly" (Hosea 5:15). The people who pray best are those who are afflicted. No wonder James was inspired to write: "Count it all joy, my brethren, when ye fall into manifold temptations [afflictions], knowing that the proving of your faith worketh patience. And let patience have its perfect work, that ye may be perfect and entire, lacking in nothing" (James 1:2-4). It is good for us to thank God, though we may not feel like it, for every affliction which brings us to our Lord in prayer.

Most people have such a full schedule and are going at such top speed that there is little or no time left for serious thinking. Affliction often takes us aside from the regular routine of life and gives us that much-needed time to think. There are those who can testify that it was during a period of affliction that they received their greatest spiritual blessings. Many have been born again in just such an atmosphere. Others have had time to take an inventory of their life, see the folly of their ways, and repent of their sins. The psalmist said, "When he slew them, then they inquired after him; and they returned and sought God earnestly. And they remembered that God was their rock, and the Most High God their redeemer" (Ps. 78:34, 35).

At a time of affliction God's Word often becomes ery precious. Affliction makes people receptive to the Word, for they find nothing else that they can hold on to. The *things* of this world then become valueless! The dross burns away, and the preciousness of God's Word stands forth. If it takes affliction to do this for us, then may affliction come! The psalmist, after a similar experience testified, "Before I was afflicted I went astray; but now I observe thy word" (Ps. 119:67).

Affliction is never to be taken lightly. "My son, regard not lightly the chastening of the Lord, nor faint when thou art reproved of him; for whom the Lord loveth he chasteneth" (Heb. 12:5, 6). David could say, "Thy rod and thy staff, they comfort me" (Ps. 23:4). Most of us can find comfort in the staff, but faint under the rod. "My brethren, these things ought not so to be." If we faint under affliction—be it sorrow, disappointment, loneliness or other losses—it is Satan's opportunity to make us hard and bitter, and thus drive us away from the Lord. On the other hand, if we accept them as from the Lord, their very pressure will cause us to become pliable in His hands.

Listen to Jonah again as he testifies: "I called by reason of mine affliction unto Jehovah." The affliction which at first seemed disastrous to Jonah and could have been his doom, turned out rather to be a great blessing. How often is not that the case! Some of God's most precious blessings are wrapped up in unattractive ways. His own Son was presented to the world in a stable, and wrapped in swaddling clothes. The afflictions which we endure may seem very unattractive and may cause us to squirm and groan, but let us remember this word of God: "All chastening seemeth for the present to be not joyous but grievous; yet *afterward* it yieldeth peaceable fruit unto them that have been exercised thereby even the fruit of righteousness" (Heb. 12:11).

24

The Outcast

"I am cast out from before thine eyes" (Jonah 2:4a).

Jonah was still praying, and his prayer at last had taken the form of a confession. It was short but to the point, for he was dying. Now for the first time he admitted he had fallen. Just think, Jonah, "the son of Amittar," had to come to the place where he classified himself as an outcast.

It takes the grace of God for a former child of God to admit that he has fallen. Adam chose rather to hide than to confess his fallen state. Israel as a nation rejected the messages of her true prophets, thinking it was impossible for her to fall out of God's grace. The Galatian church was blind to its fallen state, but the apostle Paul stated clearly, "Ye are severed from Christ . . . ye are fallen away from grace" (Gal. 5:4); "I am again in travail until Christ be formed in you" (Gal. 4:19). The Ephesian church had to get a personal letter from Christ Himself in which He bluntly told them, "Thou didst leave thy first love. Remember therefore whence thou art fallen, and repent" (Rev. 2:4, 5). What a shock to that congregation! They had already fallen, and they did not know it. To the lukewarm church of Laodicea, Jesus said, "So because thou art lukewarm, and neither hot nor cold, I will spew thee out of my mouth" (Rev. 3:16). How long do you think He will wait before He spews out lukewarm souls? How long do you wait when you have something repulsive in your mouth? Who are we today to think we can get by with the same kind of sins that caused God's saints of yesterday to fall? Oh, that all fallen sinners could see their present state! There is no help for anyone in a fallen state unless he sees and confesses his lost condition.

Satan works hard to convince fallen sinners that they have not fallen. He does not want them to realize they are outcasts, for then they might turn to God in real earnestness. Many think that because they were once baptized or had an experience of salvation, they are still saved. That is the way it should be, to be sure, but that is not always the way it works out. God's Word is clear that only those who remain in His grace retain spiritual life. All others have fallen. "As therefore ye received Christ Jesus the Lord, so walk in him, rooted and builded up in him, and established in your faith, even as ye were taught, abounding in thanksgiving" (Col. 2:6, 7). Many of the people who have been born into this world in our generation are now dead. Only those who retained the life given at birth are still alive. The same thing is true of the second birth. It is ridiculous for people to think that all is well with their souls unless they are abiding in life now. Paul urged the Corinthians, "Try your own selves, whether ye are in the faith; prove your own selves. Or know ye not as to your own selves, that Jesus Christ is in you? unless indeed ye be reprobate" (II Cor. 13:5). Of his own life, he said, "I buffet my body, and bring it into bondage; lest by any means, after that I have preached to others, I myself should be rejected" (I Cor. 9:27). If the apostle Paul feared being a castaway, how much more should we check on ourselves? Away with all deceptions of the devil on this point! May fogs and mists lift that we may see ourselves in the light of God's Word. If need be, let us confess with Jonah, "I am cast out from before thine eyes."

Jonah's confession started with the words, "I am." How would you like to finish that sentence yourself? Suppose you had but two words to choose from— saved or lost. Which one would it be? Suppose you were asked further to finish the sentence with these sets of words, choosing the one that describes you best: selfish or generous, proud or humble, hateful or loving, unhappy or joyful, worried or peaceful, impatient or patient, rough or gentle, lukewarm or hot, self-centered or Christ-centered. May the Lord give you the same grace He gave Jonah to make an honest confession of your present condition.

"I am cast out from before thine eyes." The confession is lamentable, yet what a blessing to be able to make it in the land of the living, where it can still bring results. Those very words were the turning point in Jonah's life; they may be the turning point for you. "He that covereth his transgressions shall not prosper; but whoso confesseth and forsaketh them shall obtain mercy" (Prov. 28:13).

25

Entombed

"The waters compassed me about, even to the soul; the deep was round about me; the weeds were wrapped about my head" (Jonah 2:5).

This statement is Jonah's description of his situation while he was held prisoner within the fish. The three words water, deep and weeds are the subjects of the clauses, and each in turn has a message connected with it.

I. WATER. "The waters compassed me about, even to the soul." Water is referred to in the Bible both as a blessing and as a judgment. To a thirsty land parched with scorching sun, the gentle rain from heaven is indeed a blessing. On the other hand, the swirling majestic flood waters of some mighty river are usually anything but a blessing. When Jonah said that the waters compassed him about, he was not referring to any gentle blessings from God, but rather to the terrible judgment that had befallen him. Water in this case was similar to the waters that made the flood in Noah's day.

Judgment waters leave no avenue of escape for those caught in their flow. The prophet Isaiah said, "The waters shall overflow the hiding-place" (28:

17). Places that had provided protection before are worthless when judgment waters come. Such hiding places, in fact, become coffins. The judgments of God will sweep the strongest man off his feet and carry him helplessly to his doom. There is no place for a poor victim to stand when once this mighty stream overtakes him.

Water loses no time in encompassing anything that gets in its way. In just a moment of time it can completely surround a victim and render him absolutely helpless. Jonah felt that the water had so encompassed him that even his soul, his innermost being, was saturated with it. He was trapped. The psalmist cried out in a similar experience, "Save me, O God; for the waters are come in unto my soul. I sink in deep mire, where there is no standing: I am come into deep waters, where the floods overflow me" (69:1, 2).

II. DEEP. "The deep was round about me." This second statement pictures Jonah's state as even more hopeless. Each time Jonah describes his situation, it becomes worse. This is true of all who turn their backs on God. The situation is far more serious than anyone can realize. Each time a wayward person draws his breath, his situation becomes worse. His decline is far more rapid than he realizes. "The deep" draws its victims down to a helpless condition.

When Jonah speaks of the deep, he is using very expressive language. The deep is a place where there is no human way of escape and where all sinners will ultimately find themselves. Horror, agony and regrets accompany all who go to this place. Darkness, gross darkness, darkness that penetrates the very soul, engulfs all who sink here.

Jonah, who once warned others about the wrath of God, now confessed that the deep was round about him. The best of God's servants need to have the spirit of Paul, who expressed a fear: "Lest by any means, after that I have preached to others, I myself should be rejected" (I Cor. 9:27).

III. WEEDS. "The weeds were wrapped about my head." Jonah's head, destined throughout the ages of eternity to wear the crown of life, was covered with slimy, troublesome and offensive weeds. He must have been much disturbed by them, or he would not have referred to them in this way. Jonah found himself in a "mess."

The head of an individual who disobeys the word of Jehovah is apt to be entangled in almost anything. The Christian is therefore instructed to take the helmet of salvation in order to protect his head. He that refuses to have this armor of God will soon find himself smothered with all kinds of filth of the world. A person can become so wrapped up in it that the time will come, as in Jonah's case, that he will not have strength to untangle himself.

In the words of our text, Jonah tells us where the sin of disobedience finally brought him. When he chose to go his own way, he cast his lot for a place like this. Now he had come to realize that "the wages of sin is death" (Rom. 6:23).

The amazing thing is that the Lord did not leave him in the place of his own choice. A still more wonderful thing is that our Saviour does not forsake us when we are in a similar place. The message goes out to all entombed people: "Whosoever shall call upon the name of the Lord shall be saved" (Rom. 10:13).

26

The Upward Look

"I will look again toward thy holy temple" (Jonah 2:4b).

This is the third emphatic statement that Jonah made with the pronoun I, while in the fish's belly. Usually it is a dangerous thing to talk about oneself. Jonah however, was not bragging, for he had nothing of which to brag. He had just seen himself as an outcast, and immediately he decided what to do —"I will look again toward thy holy temple."

Jonah was at last talking the language that brings results. When a helpless sinner gets to the place where he sincerely uses the words *I Will*, he means business. There is much meaning contained in those two words. It was not until David in his desperation spoke those words—"*I will* confess my transgressions unto Jehovah" (Ps. 32:5)—that the burden of his soul rolled away.

The prodigal son's new day came when he emphatically said, "*I will* arise and go to my father" (Luke 15:18). In the wedding ceremony which we use, we do not proceed to marry a couple until they have answered our questions with the words, "I will." Immediately after that, we unite them in marriage. Any sinner who comes before God and affirms the salvation covenant with the words *"I will,"* is in like manner united to his Lord. This union can never take place with a half-hearted seeker, for the promise states, "Ye shall seek me, and find me, when ye shall search for me with all your heart" (Jer. 29:13). No words can better express the attitude of a determined seeking heart than the two simple words *"I will."*

All Jonah could now do was look. "I will look again," he affirmed. He was in such a place that if deliverance depended on more, he was forever doomed. Our God has arranged it so that there is salvation in a look of faith. This truth, the snake-bitten Israelites learned when they in obedience looked at the brazen serpent. That was all that they needed to do just in simple faith, look, and they were saved. Our deliverance is similar. For "as Moses lifted up the serpent in the wilderness, even so must the Son of man be lifted up; that whosoever believeth may in him have eternal life" (John 3:14, 15).

Satan tempts people to believe that there is no hope. For three days and three nights he had Jonah believing it. If Jonah had yielded a little longer, he would have perished forever. Often it seems that Satan's last and strongest temptation for a soul seeking salvation is to make him believe he must do more than have faith in the finished work of Christ. Suppose the thief on the cross had yielded to this temptation! The poor man could not even fold his hands or bow his knees, and yet he was saved by believing in Jesus Christ. There is far more in a look of faith than we realize. Dear friend, look to Jesus.

Jonah knew where to look—"toward thy holy temple." This was his way of saying he would look to the Lord. Jonah had done a lot of looking since we first met him, but he had failed to look to God. Had he looked to God for grace to go the Nineveh road, he never would have looked for the highway that led to Joppa. Had he looked to the Lord for grace to carry him from day to day, he never would have looked for a Tarshish ship to carry him out to sea. Had he stood in God's presence and kept his eyes of faith directed on eternity's shore, he never would have stood on the ship's deck scanning the ocean for a never-to-be-reached shore of Tarshish. If he had in faith proceeded at God's command and looked for a place to preach in Nineveh, he would never have been looking for a place to sleep in the "innermost part of the ship." However, now that he was surrounded by pitch blackness, rendering his physical eyes useless, he determined to look once again to the living God. His life was nearly gone; he had only a matter of seconds left. He knew where he had received help in the past. Perhaps there was grace enough for him now. He would try once more. Therefore he said, "I *will* look again."

What a wonderful God we have! Listen to Him call, "Look unto me, and be ye saved, all the ends of the earth; for I am God, and there is none else" (Isa. 45:22). Do you feel that you are at one of these far "ends"? Take courage, dear friend, the promise is yours. Learn from Jonah that there is only one source of help. With Micah let us say, "But as for me, I will look unto Jehovah; I will wait for the God of my salvation: my God will hear me" (Micah 7:7).

27

Down to the Bottom

"I went down to the bottoms of the mountains" (Jonah 2:6).

"I went down," confessed Jonah. He could not have chosen any better words to describe how his life had been going. From the time he rebelled against the word of Jehovah there had been a continual decline. He could well have repeated the word DOWN seven times; for, as we review his life, we find at least seven downward steps.

"He went DOWN to Joppa" (1:3). This was a step of disobedience and started him in the downward direction. He preferred to do his will rather than yield to the Lord. Such decisions, which at first may seem insignificant, always lead down. Adam was the first man to learn this lesson, and since his day countless others have learned it too. Still others never seem to catch on. Jonah chose to go the hard way. He soon learned that "the wrath of God cometh upon the sons of disobedience" (Eph. 5:6).

Jonah next found a ship "and went DOWN into it" (1:3). This was a step of self-will. He was now choosing his own course. He did not say in so many words that he knew more than the Lord, but surely his actions were conveying such a belief. He did not consult the Lord to find out His will in the matter, for his mind was set to do his own will. He was going DOWN fast.

"Jonah was gone DOWN into the innermost parts of the ship; and he lay, and was fast asleep" (1:5). Jonah was here in a state of unconcern. He was soon unconscious because of sleep, and did not realize the danger about him. He was concerned about neither himself nor his fellowmen. No sleeping sinners realize the danger they or others are in; they are perfectly content just to sleep. This is the state where Satan has many people today—all such become his easy victims. It does not take long for a sinner to come down to this level. A falling object accelerates in speed as it heads downward.

The sailors "cast him forth into the sea" (1:15). Jonah was still heading down. This was a state of confusion. All who take the downward road reach this place sooner or later. He who had been destined to preach so that others could come out of confusion is now himself hurled headlong into the sea. When we refuse to heed God's command to bring the Word of God to those in darkness, it will not be long before we will be in darkness ourselves. Truly, "the way of the transgressor is hard" (Prov. 13:15).

"Jehovah prepared a great fish to swallow up Jonah" (1:17). He was swallowed "up" only to go down deeper. The ups of a runaway sinner are very slight compared to his downs. Jonah was now in the slime and filth of the fish's belly, a place of despair. He had gone so far down that he was absolutely helpless. He had never been so low before.

Not a ray of light could reach him. His head that was to have been crowned with "the helmet of salvation" was now a mass of tangled weeds. The once dignified son of Amittai, who had shunned filth of all kinds, was now wallowing in it. This is what happens to those who go DOWN.

"I went down to the bottoms of the mountains" (2:6). This was a confession of a man in a state of helplessness. Poor Jonah! He who had once been able to decide where he wanted to go was now forced to go where his sin chose to take him. He was indeed a slave of the most helpless type. A sinner who turns his back on God will some day find himself in a similar situation. There comes a time when sin so overpowers an individual that he no longer can offer any resistance. He is then carried down until he, too, comes to the very bottom— there to await eternal doom.

Six downs, and yet one to go. But can there be another? Yes, there is yet one more—eternal damnation! Jonah was already having a foretaste of it. Must he go there? No, there is a choice of another DOWN, that he had neglected from the very first. Now in utter despair and helplessness, he chose it. He got down on his knees, figuratively speaking, and cried to Jehovah for mercy. "I called by reason of mine affliction unto Jehovah" (2:2). This last DOWN should have been his first. Had he gone on his knees at the beginning of chapter one, when he was tempted to go contrary to the word of Jehovah, we would have had an altogether different story.

"I went down." These three words, we have found, are a true summary of Jonah's life. They also well describe the direction in which many people are headed today. May Jonah's lamentable confession, "I went down," call a halt to all who are going madly in his tracks! Why wait until the jaws of hell are about to swallow you DOWN forever, before falling down before the Lord and crying for mercy?

28

Memory

"I remembered Jehovah" (Jonah 2:7).

Blessed are they who have memories which the Holy Spirit can use to bring them to the Lord. Jonah had such a memory. It was his sole possession in the belly of the fish—all his other belongings were gone. But he could well afford to lose everything if he could retain such a memory. And, in fact, he had to lose everything before he discovered its blessing: "When my soul fainted within me, I remembered Jehovah."

All memory is not a blessing. It was certainly meant to be, but the Lord has warned: "If ye will not hear, and if ye will not lay it to heart, to give glory unto my name. . . . I will curse your blessings" (Mal. 2:2). What greater tragedy can happen to an individual than to have a blessing as great and as wonderful as memory, cursed! It can become then the greatest of all curses. This the rich man found out in Hades—his memory had become a torture. In answer to his plea for a drop of water, he was told, "Son, remember . . ." (Luke 16:25). Of all that he had once called his own, he had nothing left but an active, cursed memory. No doubt one of the greatest tortures of hell will be memory. Sermons and conversations that were given on this earth to lead a soul to peace will there be recalled and result in agony and despair.

Memory is meant to be a blessing. Many people have testified that they found peace with God because they recalled some portion of Scripture heard or memorized earlier in life. In Jonah's case, memory saved him from spiritual and physical death by directing him to the Lord. The psalmist said, "I remember the days of old; I meditate on all thy doings; I muse on the work of thy hands" (Psalm 143: 5). It is good for us to remind ourselves of what God has done in the past. Such memory is a great blessing and gives faith, strength and courage to a fainting heart.

Memory has an important place in all of our lives. It is the main connecting link we have with the past. In the twinkling of an eye memory can bring before us all sorts of things that happened long ago. Older people especially find much joy in memory when the twilight of life has come and they can no longer be active as before. They love to draw from memory's storehouse and recall the happy days of youth. How sad when memory must then draw from a self-centered past that has been stained with unconfessed sins. This is the reason that some old people are restless and unhappy and cannot grow old graciously. Blessed is the man whose life is Christ-centered, for his memory will then be Christ-centered too. Such a memory will be like an endless river continually bringing a flow of blessing.

Let us take inventory today of our memory's storehouse. What sort of material has it to draw from?

Will memory, when it recalls the sins of my past, also be able to recall a time when these sins were properly dealt with? Does memory have as its chief treasure an experience of salvation? Is Jesus the foremost one in my memory? Does His Word perfume the archives of my past? Will my memory, like Jonah's, have material to draw from that will lead me to my Lord in the day of trouble? These and similar questions demand an answer.

This is the day to provide material from which memory can draw. The facts that we give memory today are the ones that memory will give back to us tomorrow.

29

Consider Your Ways

"They that regard lying vanities forsake their own mercy" (Jonah 2:8)

This "sentence sermon" was nestled away in the midst of Jonah's prayer. The best sermons are those that have been conceived and born in prayer and that have come from a broken and contrite heart. Some preachers go through intense agony before a God-given message is produced. This certainly was true of Jonah. It is questionable if any preacher suffered more to bring forth a message than Jonah did with this one.

His sermon divides itself into two parts. The first part, "they that regard lying vanities," which deals with the sinner; and the second, "forsake their own mercy," which deals with the consequences of sin.

I. THE SINNER

When Jonah said, "They that regard lying vanities," he was no doubt talking about himself. He realized that he himself had been deceived by Satan to think he could run away from God. Perhaps he had been nursing some "lying vanities" that made a future in disobedience seem bright. These vanities had been blown up like a beautiful bubble, which appeared very promising and attractive until they were struck by the storm; then the bubble burst.

"Lying vanities" all come from Satan. He can make his lies look so true that even the best of people can be deceived by them. Jesus said of him, "He is a liar, and the father thereof" (John 8:44). Satan can make his lies look so attractive that the promises of God appear drab to the tempted sinner. The lies of Satan, or as Jonah calls them "lying vanities," are much more reasonable to the natural man than the eternal truths of God's Word

"Lying vanities" constitute all the false promises of Satan which we reach after but never get. For every promise of God there is at least one "lying vanity" that tries to overshadow it. To list all the "lying vanities" would be a human impossibility, but the following are some of the common ones:

Do the best you can and you will be saved.

God is too good to throw anybody into hell.

We are all headed for the same place.

There will be another chance to be saved after death.

You can sin and get by with it.

Everybody sins, so what is the difference?

Have your fling now and repent when you get old; you are too young to walk the narrow way.

If you turn your life over to Christ, you will never be happy.

You can still be a Christian and be worldly.

You are just as good as the Christians.

If you confess your sins, your life will be wrecked.

You will lose your social position if you tell others you are sorry for what you have done.

As long as you go to church, you are all right.

Such reasonings have their source in Satan, of whom Jesus said, "There is no truth in him" (John 8:44). A Christian does not dare to go by his thoughts and fancies, but he has learned to trust in God's Word. Satan can twist and warp our thoughts and feelings, but he is powerless to change the Word of God.

"Lying vanities" are Satan's trap to catch a host of careless sinners. Only the promising bait is exposed, while the destructive jaws of death, which often close at lightning speed, are cunningly concealed. When I was a boy I used to trap various kinds of fur-bearing animals. There were two principles that I always followed—one was to make the bait very attractive, and the other was to conceal the trap. On one occasion when the animals had been very cautious I put out the bait without the traps. Then when the animals were used to getting the bait, I carefully set the traps and caught them. I noticed that when once the trap had caught the victim, the bait lost its attractiveness for him. Oftentimes I could use the same bait over and over again. I used to wonder what the animals thought about as they were held in the trap waiting their doom.

Satan is a superior trapper. He is very cunning and sets his traps well. He is out to get souls that have been purchased with the precious blood of Christ. Every twenty-four hours his death-traps take an appalling toll.

Dear reader, are you by any chance lured by some "lying vanity"? If a prophet like Jonah could be deceived, surely it behooves us to check on ourselves. It is tragic indeed if we are this day reaching after the juicy promises of "lying vanity" and are unaware of the trap that is about to catch us. Let us heed God's warning, "There is a way which seemeth right unto a man; but the end thereof are the ways of death" (Prov. 14:12 and 16:25).

II. THE CONSEQUENCES OF SIN

The second part of Jonah's sermon tells of the consequences of sin. Sinners, said Jonah, "forsake their own mercy." Jonah knew what he was preaching about, for this sermon was not mere theory that he had hatched in his brain. Ah, no, he had experienced this very thing. He had himself been guilty of "forsaking his own mercy" by turning his back on God. "The way of a fool is right in his own eyes" (Prov. 12:15). Jonah had been a fool.

All who regard "lying vanities" do so at the cost of forsaking mercy. The price is stupendous. Such sinners are as foolish as a drowning man who exchanges a lifesaver for a cement block. He exchanges life for death. To forsake mercy means to throw away one's salvation. But, some may ask, can a human being be so foolish? The answer is yes, for it is actually done every day. There will no doubt be some readers of these lines who have already forsaken their own mercy. Surely then, you may again say, such people must be full of fear over their lost condition. To that we must answer, "No." The "lying vanities" have so deceived them that they can lightly scan these lines and not be disturbed. The hypnotic power of him who spins out the "lying vanities" keeps his subjects in such a stupor that they are blinded to their own fate. That was the way it worked with Jonah, and that is the way it still works.

"Mercy" is the avenue by which we poor sinners can return to God. The publican came that way when he smote his breast and cried, "God, be thou merciful to me a sinner" (Luke 18:13). Let us never forget that "according to his *mercy* he saved us" (Titus 3:5). Anyone who forsakes the mercy of God is committing spiritual suicide. He cuts off his only avenue of escape and seals his own doom.

Not until there has been a denouncing of "lying vanities" can there be a returning to mercy, for it is impossible to have both. Those who choose lying vanities forsake their own mercy, but those who turn to mercy forsake lying vanities. We have our choice of either believing the Word of God or else reaching for vain lies; the one belongs to God, the other belongs to the devil. Jesus gave us a timely warning in this matter when He said, "No man can serve two masters; for either he will hate the one, and love the other; or else he will hold to one, and despise the other. Ye cannot serve God and mammon" (Matt. 6:24).

Jonah's sermon is over. It took him less than five seconds to preach it, but its truth will live on forever. His message has found its way to us, and in so doing demands a response. What is your answer?

Let us take to heart the refrain from the prophet Haggai, "Consider your ways" (Haggai 1:5, 7).

30

Thanksgiving

"I will sacrifice unto thee with the voice of thanksgiving" (Jonah 2:9).

Jonah was not sitting on a swivel chair by a highly polished desk when he worded this thanksgiving proclamation. Rather, he was gasping for breath amidst the slime and filth of the fish's belly. This seemed to be a queer time to hold a thanksgiving service. Usually we think of thanksgiving following a time of great material blessings. We then try to enumerate all that we have received from the Lord and say a grateful "thank you." Jonah had just the opposite setting for his time of thanksgiving. He had just undergone a series of great losses.

Jonah had lost all his friends. Not one living soul could join him in this thanksgiving service. It was really pathetic. The sailors who had been so considerate of him a few days previous were no doubt safely back on shore now, relaxing after their harrowing experience. Jonah was alone. As he experienced the feelings of loneliness, he proclaimed a thanksgiving service.

Jonah missed his desired destination. His ambition was to reach Tarshish; therefore, he had put forth both money and effort to get there. Now because of outward circumstances his plans were suddenly interrupted. It is not easy to have one's plans suddenly changed. Once a person sets his heart to reach a desired goal, he finds it a great disappointment if anything interferes with that plan. Have you ever been in a situation like that? Did it ever dawn upon you that at that very time in the midst of disappointment and even great loss, thanksgiving would be in order?

Jonah also lost his possessions. We do not know how much he took with him on this journey; but usually, when a person makes a long trip, he carries a substantial wardrobe. We do not know whether the sailors tossed his belongings into the sea after him or if they were washed overboard by the storm. In either event Jonah lost them. Everything he had taken with him when he tried to run away from the Lord was lost forever. As far as we can tell, he lost everything he once owned; yet he was proclaiming a thanksgiving service. Have you ever realized that the loss of material possessions is an occasion to begin thanking God? Jonah's experience underscores a familiar truth. The more a man loses, the more thankful he is for what still remains. A person may have perfect health and not be thankful for it. Let him lose it and regain but a part, and he will be more thankful for the little regained than for the much he once had. Our nature is very ungrateful. Too often we have to lose what we have in order to appreciate it.

Then, too, we often have to lose our material blessings in order to appreciate the spiritual. This was the case with Jonah. When he had lost everything, he "remembered Jehovah." He realized that he still had the best left, for he had his Lord. He had therefore much for which to be thankful. When this truth dawned on him, he determined: "I will sacrifice unto thee with the voice of thanksgiving."

A thanksgiving service is always in order. The trouble with many of us is that we think thanksgiving should be given only when material wealth has come our way. Jonah has something to teach here. We are admonished in Scripture to come into God's presence with thanksgiving. "Let us come before his presence WITH THANKSGIVING" (Psalm 95:2). Again, "In nothing be anxious; but in everything by prayer and supplication WITH THANKSGIVING let your requests be made known unto God" (Phil. 4:6). Is that the way you burst into God's presence? Is it not easier to come moaning and groaning with a lot of requests? All our prayers are to be spiced with thanksgiving. We are told to "continue stedfastly in prayer, watching therein WITH THANKS-GIVING" (Col. 4:2).

When a distressed soul declares a thanksgiving service, he is close to the time of his release. Paul and Silas declared a thanksgiving service while in their darkest hour in the Philippian jail. They had every reason to be discouraged; still they praised God. It was only a matter of hours after this before they were free. They had literally praised their way to freedom. Jehoshaphat, the king of Judah, won his greatest victory when he gave orders to his soldiers that they "should sing unto Jehovah, and give praise in holy array " (II Chron. 20:21). They used as their theme song, "Give thanks unto Jehovah; for his lovingkindness endureth forever." Victory followed immediately. Release was close to Jonah when he came to the place where he could thank God in these dark circumstances. Release awaits anyone who will begin to thank and praise God amid discouraging surroundings.

Does this day find you in dark circumstances? Do not forget God has promised "with the temptation" to "make also the way of escape" (I Cor. 10:13). Learn from Jonah. Proclaim a thanksgiving service. Let discouragement, sorrow, poverty, sickness, helplessness and hopelessness be a reminder to say with Jonah, "I will sacrifice unto thee with the voice of thanksgiving."

31

Vows

"I will pay that which I have vowed" (Jonah 2:9).

This is the seventh and last statement in which Jonah used the personal pronoun I while he was in the fish. There has been a steady progress of hope from the first time when he confessed, "I called by reason of mine affliction" (2:2), until this time. It seems that seven has become a favorite number with Jonah. We traced his seven downward steps, and now we have listened to his seven confessions, which we could also call upward steps. He has one confession for each step down. In both cases it was his seventh and last step that brought results.

Jonah here confessed his besetting sin. He admitted that he had failed because he had not kept his promise. Notice that he did not say, "I will continue to pay my vow," but "I will pay." By this statement he admitted that he had failed in the past and that he would now make the thing right.

Jonah is at last confessing the initial sin which had led him into all his other sins. Woe be to any man who does not keep his word with God. He is certain to have rough going with every step he takes leading him deeper into sin. God cannot be mocked. A promise to Him must be kept. "When thou shalt vow a vow unto the Lord thy God, thou shalt not be slack to pay it: for the Lord thy God will surely require it of thee; and it would be sin in thee" (Deut. 23:21).

Jonah also indirectly confesses that Jehovah is faithful. He puts no blame on Him. He rather likens Jehovah to a faithful mate waiting for the deserter to return. If Jehovah were as faithless as we are, it would be of no use for us to return and pay that which we have vowed. There would be no one to whom to return! Thank God that the Scriptures compare our God to the father of the prodigal son who was always looking and waiting for his wayward son to return. What a sad story it would have been had the prodigal come home and found a father who no longer loved him; again, how sad if the home had been sold and the father moved to some unknown place. Scripture, however, wants to impress us with the facts that the father remained faithful even though the son was unfaithful, and that it was at the same place where the son had left his father that he was again reunited with him. "If we are faithless, he abideth faithful; for he cannot deny himself" (II Tim. 2:13). May we never forget that God is faithful!

Jonah knew the way back to God. He took that way—the only way—confessing his besetting sin. Had Jonah wished, he could have confessed numerous other sins and still not found release. But he had no time to waste, so he confessed that sin at once. God has promised, "If we confess our sins, he is faithful and righteous to forgive us our sins, and to cleanse us from all unrighteousness" (I John 1:9). If we confess the sins of which God is convicting us, He promises to forgive us. But that is not all. He also promises "to cleanse us from all unrighteousness." God never partially forgives a sinner. He knows that our attitude toward our initial sins will also be our attitude toward all the rest of our sins. If we are willing to confess the sins which He points out, He will cleanse us from these "AND all unrighteousness." Therefore it behooves a burdened sinner to deal with the sins that the Holy Spirit reveals. Too often burdened souls will confess dozens of other sins and still not find peace. Let us learn from Jonah, and at any cost confess the sin or sins of which the Holy Spirit is convicting.

Jonah wanted to get back to the right starting place. In order to do so, he had to go back before the time of our acquaintance with him. He went back to the time when in simple childlike faith he promised to be faithful to His Lord. He recalled with joy that blessed day when his heart was full of devotion to his God, and when he vowed to be faithful. This brought him back to his original starting place. Here he found solid footing and could start all over again.

How far Jonah had to go back we do not know. The important question now is how far some wayward reader may have to go back to get solid footing. Some will need to return to the day of their confirmation when they vowed to be faithful; others, to some particular moment in their life when they made great promises. There are those who may need to go back to promises made at a time of great need, perhaps at a time of sickness or when death called some loved one. Pray for grace to go back far enough to find solid footing! Let God's own Word call you back. "Return, thou backsliding Israel . . . I will not look in anger upon you; for I am merciful, saith Jehovah, I will not keep anger for ever. Only acknowledge thine iniquity, that thou hast transgressed against Jehovah thy God . . . and ye have not obeyed my voice . . . Return, O backsliding children" (Jer. 3:12-14).

32

Salvation

"Salvation is of Jehovah" (Jonah 2:9).

This was the last statement of Jonah's prayer. It had taken him a long time to come to this conclusion. Experience had taught him that salvation was not in good works. If good works could have saved him, the husky sailors would have succeeded in getting him back to safety. He realized further that salvation was not in his own efforts; for, no matter what he tried, he was still entombed in the fish's belly. At last the greatest truth that can ever dawn upon a lost soul came to him. He saw that if ever he were to be saved, it must come from Jehovah.

This great truth, "Salvation is of Jehovah," is not easy to see. There is no truth that Satan tries to hide so much as this one. "The god of this world [Satan] hath blinded the minds of the unbelieving, that the light of the gospel of the glory of Christ, who is the image of God, should not dawn upon them" (II Cor. 4:4). Satan is untiring in his efforts to cause unbelief to prevail in the hearts of his captives. Knowing that "belief cometh of hearing, and hearing by the word of Christ" (Rom. 10:17), and that the "word of God is living and active" (Heb. 4:12), Satan greatly fears that unbelievers might hear the Word of God. Therefore his greatest concern is to keep them away from the influence of that Word. This explains why people find it so hard to read the Bible, or to come to places where God's Word is preached in its truth and purity. All witnesses who have any part in proclaiming that "salvation is of Jehovah" are in direct line with the heaviest attacks of Satan.

"Salvation is of Jehovah" is a truth that has freed many a struggling soul. Martin Luther worked for years to free himself before he saw this truth in the words, "The righteous shall live by faith" (Rom. 1:17). Jesus said, "Ye shall know the truth, and the truth shall make you free" (John 8:32). If we were to go to individuals who have been set free from the bondage of sin and ask them who set them free, they would say, "Jesus Christ." If we should ask them how, they would answer that it was through some portion of God's Word. If we further pressed them for the particular passage, we would get varied answers. Perhaps no two would be alike, for all of God's Word is the "incorruptible seed" through which souls are "begotten again" (I Peter 1:23). In the case of Jonah, too, he at last turned to God's Word. It could well be he was thinking of Psalm 3:8, "Salvation belongeth unto Jehovah," or it may have been Psalm 37:39, "The salvation of the righteous is of Jehovah." It does not matter so much which particular passage it was—he had laid hold of the eternal truth, that "Salvation is of Jehovah."

Notice that no release came to Jonah until he saw that salvation was from God. No one ever gets any permanent release until he sees and trusts this truth. Jonah's prayer ended with this statement that "salvation is of Jehovah," and the next statement tells us about his release. Release always comes after we get our eyes on our Lord. When Jonah talked about salvation, he touched the most tender part of the Lord's heart. Our Lord has no greater joy than that of saving some poor soul. We would therefore make a plea to all struggling souls that they look to the Lord first for salvation. Had Jonah done that, he would have saved himself much grief. Many of God's faithful followers today can confess that they, too, were groping in the dark until their eyes were opened to see that "salvation is of Jehovah." The psalmist was so desperate he cried out to the Lord, "Say unto my soul, I am thy salvation" (Psalm 35:3).

"Salvation is of Jehovah" was not only the closing word of Jonah's prayer, but also his personal testimony. We heard his seven confessions and now in four simple words we have his testimony. Notice it was all Jehovah-centered; Jonah did not say a word about himself. Such testimonies please the Lord. Can anybody give a better one in so few words? Suppose you were asked to give your testimony, could you with conviction say with Jonah, "Salvation is of Jehovah"?

33

Deliverance

"And Jehovah spake unto the fish, and it vomited out Jonah upon the dry land" (Jonah 2:10).

Jonah's day of deliverance had come. The fish that had entombed him for three long days suddenly had to let him go.

Jonah's deliverance came because of the word of the Lord. It was not until "Jehovah spake unto the fish" that the miracle happened. No sinner, wherever imprisoned, will ever get free apart from God's Word. When Jesus ministered to sinners, it was always His word that gave them freedom. It was the words, "Thy sins are forgiven thee" (Luke 7:48) that gave deliverance to the sinful woman who wept at His feet. It was the same words that gave release to the man sick of palsy (Matt. 9:2). Jesus said to His disciples, "Ye are clean because of the word which I have spoken unto you" (John 15:3).

In our day we have God's recorded Word which can set any sinner free. Its pages are full of promises that can perform miracles. God is waiting for imprisoned individuals to lay hold of them. "He hath granted unto us his precious and exceeding great promises; that through these ye may become partakers of the divine nature" (II Pet. 1:4).

If Jehovah could speak to a carefree sea monster and make it deliver Jonah upon dry land, can He not speak to any monster that may have you in its grip and cause a deliverance? The monsters of ill-temper, carelessness, hate, evil thoughts, jealousy, impatience, lust, fornication and drunkenness are bulging with the many victims they have swallowed. If any of these have a hold on you, pray now for deliverance.

Remember, all your trying will not save you any more than Jonah's trying saved him. Jonah had to come to the conclusion that "salvation is of Jehovah" before there could be any deliverance. Simply cast yourself upon the Lord and cry out, "God, be merciful to me a sinner" (Luke 18:13). Then ask for grace to believe in Jesus as He says, "Him that cometh to me I will in no wise cast out." Jesus is ready to give you complete deliverance now. He can make a modern Jonah out of you.

Jonah was delivered upon dry land. The Lord arranged it so that he was to have a place of solid footing. What a tragedy if Jonah had been delivered out of the fish while in mid-ocean. However, God does not deliver people that way. He sets them on solid ground so that they can get a good start to go on His errands. The psalmist testified of his deliverance in these words: "He brought me up also out of a horrible pit, out of the miry clay; and he set my feet upon a rock, and established my goings. And he hath put a new song in my mouth, even praise unto our God" (Ps. 40:2, 3).

We have now come to the close of chapter two

and find that this chapter also ends with the mercy of Jehovah. Our God delights to show mercy; for He is "merciful and gracious, slow to anger, and abundant in loving kindness and truth" (Ex. 34:6).

34

God Calling Yet

"And the word of Jehovah came unto Jonah the second time" (Jonah 3:1).

The third chapter of Jonah gives an account of the great awakening that took place in Nineveh. This awakening took on such vast proportions that it stands out as one of the greatest recorded in the Bible. There is no other reference to this great awakening other than the words of Jesus, "The men of Nineveh shall stand up in judgment with this generation, and shall condemn it: for they repented at the preaching of Jonah; and behold, a greater than Jonah is here" (Luke 11:32).

There are at least seven important things about the Nineveh revival that we shall consider. The first is that God must have a man to preach His word. Just how much time elapsed from the day of Jonah's deliverance until his second call from God came, we do not know. It is interesting to notice that the Lord waited until Jonah was back in normal surroundings before He called him. The Lord did not use any "high pressure" methods to force Jonah into service. Had He wanted to, He could have given Jonah this second call while he was entombed in the fish, telling him, "You either go to Nineveh or else."

But the Lord does not do things that way. He does not force anyone into His service, but calls gently, and gives each one ample opportunity to either accept or reject.

Although Jonah had utterly failed the first time, he was again offered an opportunity to serve God. Many of God's successful followers have once been failures. The apostle Peter once cursed and swore, denying that he had ever known Christ. However, after he had repented with bitter tears, he was permitted to continue as the leader of the apostles and was given the honor of preaching the Pentecost sermon that won 3,000 people for Christ.

David utterly failed his God when he fell into the sins of adultery and murder. He, too, after repentance and restoration, was allowed to continue as God's chosen servant.

Because an individual has failed is no excuse for him to forsake God's call. Rather, failure, if dealt with in the right way, can be turned into blessing, for "we know that to them that love God all things work together for good, even to them that are called according to his purpose" (Rom. 8:28).

The Lord could have let Jonah die in his plight and called some other less stubborn man to go and preach in his place. However, in His patience and compassion for sinners He deals with the erring not according to what they deserve, but according to His own lovingkindness. That is the way He is dealing with sinners today. If He should suddenly change His method, there would be no hope for any of us. "He hath not dealt with us after our sins, nor rewarded us after our iniquities" (Ps. 103:10), for "Jehovah is merciful and gracious, slow to anger, and abundant in lovingkindness" (Ps. 103:8).

The Lord is still calling. He is calling some to salvation and others to service. All of us have wasted valuable time in the past. Not a moment now should be lost. This may be our last call before the angel of death gives us the final summons.

Regardless of how much we have been stained by our sinful past, let us be obedient now. Let us, by God's grace, say with the apostle Paul, "One thing I do, forgetting the things which are behind, and stretching forward to the things which are before, I press on toward the goal unto the prize of the high calling of God in Christ Jesus" (Phil. 3:13, 14).

God calling yet! Shall I not hear?
Earth's pleasures shall I still hold dear?
Shall life's swift passing years all fly,
And still my soul in slumber lie?

God calling yet! Shall I not rise?
Can I His loving voice despise,
And basely His kind care repay?
He calls me still, can I delay?

Ah, yield Him all: in Him confide.
Where but with Him doth peace abide?
Break loose, let earthly bonds be riven,
And let the spirit rise to heaven!

God calling yet! I cannot stay,
My heart I yield without delay;
Vain world, farewell! from thee I part;
The voice of God hath reached my heart!
                                    —GERHARD TERSTEEGEN

35

"The Preaching That I Bid Thee"

"Arise, go to Nineveh that great city and preach unto it the preaching that I bid thee" (Jonah 3:2).

The second step in the Nineveh revival is that God's Word was to be preached. Jonah was instructed, "Preach unto it the preaching that I bid thee" (Jonah 3:2).

No awakenings come apart from God's Word. They always come as a result of the Word. The Word of God is the "incorruptible seed" (I Peter 1:23) that alone gives life which can result in an awakening. "He hath granted unto us his precious and exceeding great promises; that through these ye may become partakers of the divine nature" (II Peter 1:4). The power lies in the Word. "For the word of God is living" (Heb. 4:12). The apostle Paul, knowing that life is imparted through the Word of God, admonished his young partner Timothy to "Preach the Word" (II Tim. 4:2). The Lord Himself has said, "Is not my word like fire . . . and like a hammer that breaketh the rock in pieces?" (Jer. 23:29). Therefore all awakenings whether in an

122

individual's life or in a community must come as a result of contact with God's Word.

Bible history bears witness to this truth. In the days when King Josiah came to the throne of Judah, the people were paying little or no attention to God's Word. One day the King decided to have the temple cleaned and repaired. It was during this remodeling program that an old copy of "the book of the law" was found in the rubbish. When this was read in the presence of the king, the power of God's Word took immediate effect. "He rent his clothes" and said, "Great is the wrath of Jehovah that is kindled against us because our fathers have not hearkened unto the words of this book to do according to all that which is written concerning us" (II Kings 22:13). These sincere words were the introduction to a great material and spiritual blessing for the nation.

The awakening that started with the conversion of 3000 people at Pentecost also came as a direct result of the preaching of the Word of God. A short simple handling of God's Word caused the listening people to be "pricked in their heart" and cry out, "Brethren, what shall we do" (Acts 2:37). Salvation, whether it comes to one or to many, always and with no exception comes through the use of God's Word.

Men who have been successful soul-winners have learned to give God's Word its rightful place. The apostles at one time prayed, "Grant unto thy servants to speak thy word with all boldness while thou stretchest forth thy hand to heal; and that signs and wonders may be done through the name of thy holy servant Jesus" (Acts 4:29-30). Note that all they asked for themselves was "to speak thy word with boldness." They could have asked for many other things at this particular time, such as safety, success, or happiness. But they knew the importance of the Word and had learned to trust in its power. They had learned the secret that all they needed was to preach rightfully the Word of God, and the Lord would do the rest. They were well acquainted with the promise concerning God's Word, "It shall not return unto me void, but it shall accomplish that which I please, and it shall prosper in the thing whereto I sent it" (Isa. 55:11).

Notice that Jonah was instructed to preach "the preaching that I bid thee." He was not only to preach the Word of God, but he must preach the right word for the occasion. God's Word can be spoken in such a way that it becomes limited because it fails to fit the occasion. Job's friends are an example of this. When they came to console him, they said some wonderful things about God, but they were later sharply rebuked by God himself, "for ye have not spoken of me the thing that is right" (Job 42:7). A doctor must not only give medicine but he must give the right kind of medicine. What is good for one occasion may prove disastrous at another. Thus the servant of the Lord must always be relying on the Holy Spirit to bring to his remembrance exactly the right word. There can be no cut-and-dried system for soul-winning.

There has been much talk about awakenings and revivals in our day. All this talk is worthless unless God's Word is given its rightful place in our lives. It would be better if we laid our emphasis not on revival or awakening, much as we need them, but rather on the rightful use of God's Word. In time this will result in awakenings and revivals.

The crying need today is to get messengers who will deliver the message without tampering with it, men who are so in touch with God that they can get His Word from Him and will deliver it at any cost, men who "will preach . . . the preaching that I bid thee." This is one step in an awakening. If you are a child of God and desire to be such a messenger, volunteer to Him. Use the words of Isaiah, "Here am I, send me." (Isaiah 6:8).

36

Faith

"And the people of Nineveh believed God" (Jonah 3:5).

The first important step in the Nineveh awakening, as we have mentioned, was the calling of a man to preach. The second step was the preaching of the Word of God. The third step was the faith that sprang forth from the hearts of the people after they had listened to the preaching of the Word. When Jonah had proclaimed his judgment message, the people believed it. There is never an awakening, whether in an individual life or in a community, apart from faith—faith in God's Word.

Faith is a short word but very important. "Without faith it is impossible to be well-pleasing unto God" (Heb. 11:6). Salvation can be given only to those who have faith, "For by grace have ye been saved through *faith;* and that not of yourselves, it is the gift of God" (Eph. 2:8). Jesus said to the sinful woman seeking forgiveness, "Thy *faith* hath saved thee; go in peace" (Luke 7:50). To the woman with the issue of blood He said, "Thy *faith* hath made thee whole; go in peace" (Luke 8:48). Faith and God's children cannot be separated. In Hebrews 11 where a part of the list of God's "Who's Who" in heaven is mentioned, we see that every one of them is there because of his faith.

Faith in Christ is the most valuable possession a person can have. Without it eternity's blessings are forever lost; with it all the blessings of heaven are freely given. When the apostle Paul came to the last days of his life and took inventory of what he still had, he could victoriously say, "I have kept the faith" (II Tim. 4:7). He still had his most valuable possession. Blessed be those who go through life retaining a child-like faith. There is nothing of which Satan and his demons would rather rob a child of God than his faith. Jude, one of the New Testament writers, urged all his readers to "contend earnestly for the faith which was once for all delivered unto the saints" (Jude v. 3). Jesus said that He would look for faith when He returns to this earth. "When the Son of man cometh, shall he find faith on the earth?" (Luke 18:8). True faith at that time will be rare. There will no doubt be much religious and church activity, but that alone is not what Jesus wants. He wants faith—simple faith in Him—faith like that found in Nineveh after Jonah had preached.

The people of Nineveh "believed God." Not a word is said about their faith in Jonah. The Word of God had been preached in such a way that it was God with whom they were dealing. Jonah to them was like a messenger-boy who had delivered the message and withdrawn. They were concerned not with the messenger but with the message. When this happens to a people, another step has been taken that will eventually result in an awakening.

Let us take note of what the Ninevites believed.

The message that Jonah had to proclaim was one of doom and judgment. "Yet forty days and Nineveh shall be overthrown" (v. 4). There wasn't any gospel in that message. Yet we read that the people believed it. Such messages are not easy to accept. Noah had a similar proclamation in his day, but the people refused to believe it. The prophets who witnessed to Israel and Judah came with similar messages, but their words were rejected. In our day, too, the message is given that "the elements shall be dissolved with fervent heat, and the earth and the works that are therein shall be burned up" (II Peter 3:10), but most people ignore this warning.

People love to accept what is pleasant and disregard the unpleasant. They often accept what the Word of God has to say about heaven but refuse to believe there is a hell. They gather to themselves the promises of God but reject His warnings. They will even accept the part of a verse that appeals to them and ignore the rest that does not suit their fancy. The people of Nineveh, however, were not so, for they "believed God."

Let us note the kind of people who had faith. They were raw heathen who before had known little or nothing about God. The Word of God was unknown to them except for the meagre information that might have trickled out of Israel and Judah. They were so steeped in sin of the grossest kind that their wickedness called for a hasty judgment. God had given them but forty days in which to repent. These people, who were the enemy of Israel, now "believed God." Truly a great miracle had taken place. It is always a miracle when any sinner is given grace to believe God.

There is a great lesson that this text would teach us. Little do we know what will happen to the most hopeless people if they are confronted with God's Word. History has recorded over and over again how the hardest and most rebellious people have had to yield when they came face to face with God's Word. Faith has been kindled in the most unexpected hearts and in the most unexpected places. Let us then take courage; for God reigns, and we are still living in the day of grace. Take to heart the words of God spoken through the prophet, "I am working a work in your day, which ye will not believe though it be told you" (Hab. 1:5).

37

Repentance

"The people of Nineveh believed God; and they proclaimed a fast, and put on sackcloth, from the greatest of them even to the least of them" (Jonah 3:5).

True faith always results in action, for "faith, if it have not works, is dead in itself" (Jas. 2:17). In the case of the people of Nineveh, faith resulted in repentance—repentance that was genuine. We shall consider the subject of repentance as the fourth step in the Nineveh awakening.

True repentance is a gift from God and belongs to His abundant grace. The apostle Paul admonished his partner, Timothy, so to conduct himself in the presence of the people that "peradventure God may give them repentance" (II Tim. 2:25). The apostles also brought out this truth when they said of Jesus, "Him did God exalt with his right hand to be a Prince and a Saviour, to give repentance to Israel, and remission of sins" (Acts 5:31). When they were discussing the conversion of Cornelius they said, "Then to the Gentiles also hath God granted repentance unto life" (Acts 11:18). In these references we see that repentance does not come from us as individuals, but is a blessing that God Himself gives. Then it would be in order for any soul to pray for grace to repent, remembering that it is "the goodness of God" that "leadeth thee to repentance."

Much so-called repentance is not genuine. It may resemble the real thing so closely as to deceive many. Tears may be shed, confessions made and even a reformation follow, but still this may not be repentance. Wicked Pharaoh confessed, "I have sinned this time: Jehovah is righteous, and I and my people are wicked" (Ex. 9:27); yet he never repented. Judas who betrayed Christ confessed, "I betrayed innocent blood" (Mt. 27:4); yet these remorseful words did not lead to real repentance. Scripture speaks of such remorse as the "sorrow of the world" which "worketh death" (II Cor. 7:10). Many people feel sorry that their sins have been exposed, and they find a release in admitting them. To be sure, they thus have some sort of an "experience," but this is not repentance. They do not confess as David of old, "Against thee [God], thee only, have I sinned" (Ps. 51:4). We do much harm by not discerning between genuine and false repentance. In our desire to "see results" we are in danger of labeling anyone who sheds a few tears as repentant. Since true repentance is so precious, the evil one will counterfeit it; and, unless we receive our enlightenment from the Holy Spirit, we shall be deceived.

True repentance means a complete turn-about. To be sorry for sin and then to continue in it is not repentance, for "Know ye not, that to whom ye present yourselves as servants unto obedience, his servants ye are whom ye obey; whether of sin unto death, or of obedience unto righteousness?" (Rom

6:16). When the Corinthian church actually repented of their sin, the apostle summed up their behavior in a few words that give us a good definition of true repentance: "What earnest care it wrought in you, yea what clearing of yourselves, yea what indignation, yea what fear, yea what longing, yea what zeal, yea what avenging! In everything ye approved yourselves to be pure in the matter" (II Cor. 7:11). Truly, this was a "godly sorrow" working "repentance unto salvation, a repentance which bringeth no regret" (II Cor. 7:10). The people of Nineveh followed this pattern, for the decree was made, "Yea, let them turn every one from his evil way, and from the violence that is in his hands" (Jonah 3:8). There was a complete change. This was genuine repentance. Whereas they had been headed away from God, they now turned toward Him. This turning around and heading in the opposite direction is repentance.

Repentance is very important. The Lord Jesus gave orders that "repentance and remission of sins should be preached in his name unto all the nations" (Luke 24:47). There can be no salvation apart from repentance. People must be told to repent. John the Baptist's voice rang out over the wilderness of Judea, "Repent ye; for the kingdom of heaven is at hand" (Mt. 3:2). Jesus Himself came preaching, "Repent ye, and believe in the gospel" (Mark 1:15). The apostles directed the people, "Repent ye therefore, and turn again, that your sins may be blotted out, that so there may come seasons of refreshing from the presence of the Lord" (Acts 3:19). The apostle Paul, in giving a summary of his work at Ephesus, said that he had testified "both to Jews

132

and to Greeks repentance toward God, and faith toward our Lord Jesus Christ" (Acts 20:21). Down through the ages the note of repentance has been sounded by all God's faithful servants.

Repentance is the one step that stands between countless numbers of people and salvation. Many want the blessings of God but hesitate to go the way of repentance. There have been many substitutes for repentance, but God accepts none of them. The road of repentance alone leads to eternal life. That way is still open. Let us learn from the people of Nineveh that it is time to call a halt. May we pray, "Search me, O God, and know my heart; try me, and know my thoughts; and see if there be any wicked way in me, and lead me in the way everlasting" (Ps. 139:23, 24).

38

Repentance Leads to Action

"And the tidings reached the king of Nineveh, and he arose from his throne, and laid his robe from him, and covered him with sackcloth, and sat in ashes" (Jonah 3:6)

The spirit of a true awakening is contagious. It spreads rapidly and affects all classes of people. This was true of the Nineveh awakening, for it started with "the greatest of them" and reached "even to the least of them" (v. 5). We will consider here, as the fourth step in the Nineveh awakening, the winning of "the greatest of them," the king of Nineveh himself, with whom the awakening started.

This influential leader became the key man in the awakening. He was in a position to be either the greatest hindrance or the greatest promoter of God's work—he chose the latter. It was he who "made proclamation and published through Nineveh" (v. 7) that there should be a turning to God. It is interesting to notice that of all the people of Nineveh, the king was the only one singly mentioned. His conversion and testimony must have been of vital importance since Scripture made room for this to be recorded.

Our introduction to the king comes after Jonah had started his preaching mission in Nineveh. Then "the tidings reached the king." One never knows how far a Holy Spirit-inspired message will go. God has said that His Word "shall not return unto me void, but it shall accomplish that which I please, and it shall prosper in the thing whereto I sent it" (Isa. 55:11). When Jonah went to proclaim his message, he must have been conscious of the king of Nineveh. Perhaps the very thought of him filled Jonah with fear. But it was God's will that the word Jonah preached should eventually be relayed to the king himself. How this was done we do not know. It is enough for us to know that "the tidings reached the king." God has ways of promoting His Word far beyond what His followers can "ask or think." When "the preaching that I bid thee" (v. 2) goes forth, God Himself will see to it that it eventually reaches the desired destination.

The results of God's Word upon this key man were beyond all expectation. He who had ruled Nineveh when their wickedness had called for God's judgment now "arose from his throne." He who had always given orders to others was now willing to yield to orders himself. He was willing to relinquish his seat of authority and submit to a greater authority. No human being could have made the king of Nineveh do this. It would have taken armies upon armies to dethrone him, for there is no place a king cherishes so much as his throne. He will die defending it. But all it took to dethrone the king of Nineveh was the simple preaching of God's Word. No wonder he became a key man in the awakening. God is willing to use anyone who will relinquish the throne of his heart and yield full authority to Him. In fact, it is only such "dethroned" people that He can use. There would be many more key people and many more awakenings today if there were more "throne" surrenders.

The king also "laid his robe from him." He no doubt had many robes. We can think of them as a beautiful covering for the wicked self-life. He had taken every precaution to see to it that his wicked old self was well covered with the most beautiful robes. The king undoubtedly valued these royal robes next to his throne, for it was while he was dressed in them that his subjects paid him respect and honor. But in this solemn hour, when God's wrath was about to be poured out, "robes" of this nature seemed useless for protection. The tidings that had reached the king called for disrobing. He stripped himself of all his former coverings, until he was on the level of the poorest sinner in Nineveh, and stood before the Lord as he actually was. God uses "disrobed" people today, too.

The king also "covered him with sackcloth." What do you suppose the attendants thought who helped him wrap himself in this drab covering? They had never in all their experience in a king's court seen anything like this. No one had ever stalked the rooms of the palace in such a dress. But the tidings that the king had heard had made him conscious of his sins. His heart was heavy because of his past life and he would dress accordingly—in the sackcloth of the repentant sinner. Sackcloth was not a popular dress, but the king broke all conventions in his humiliation. Because he humbled himself, God could use him; "God resisteth the proud, but giveth grace to the humble" (James 4:6).

The king also "sat in ashes." He who had always been given the best seat now chose to sit on an ash pile. Imagine the contrast—from a throne to an ash pile, from the most exalted seat in the kingdom to the humblest place of all. The news of such an act must have spread quickly. What a sight for the people of Nineveh to behold! It must have given them a shock that well prepared them for the proclamation that followed. Every true awakening has with it these unexpected shocks. Perhaps the king feared as he humiliated himself that his subjects would despise him. If so, his fears were not worth recording, for we find no reference to them. Such fears are from the evil one and have no value for good. This was not a time for the king to be concerned about what people thought of him. He, as well as his people had sinned, and God's judgment was about to strike. He wasn't ready to face God and therefore chose this humble place seeking mercy. All true awakenings have their ash piles. God always chooses His workers from this place.

Whenever a person acts in obedience to God's Word, the cause of the kingdom moves on with accelerated speed. "God is no respecter of persons." Though the king of Nineveh had once been a champion of wickedness, he now became the key man to lead people to repentance. God is still looking for men like the king of Nineveh—key men—who can be used to promote His cause. Do you happen to know where He can find one?

39

An Urgent Proclamation

"Let neither man nor beast, herd nor flock, taste anything; let them not feed, nor drink water; but let them be covered with sackcloth, both man and beast, and let them cry mightily unto God" (Jonah 3:7, 8).

The above statement is the call of the king of Nineveh for an all-out prayer meeting. His subjects had received many proclamations from him, but never before anything like this. When this command reached them, they realized that prayer was important. Prayer is indeed far more important than any of us realize. Every awakening, large or small, has its roots in a prayer meeting. It does not surprise us then to find prayer as a contributory factor to the Nineveh awakening.

Prayer was given its rightful place in Nineveh. It came first. The command that came from the king stated that even food and drink, the necessities of everyday living, were now to be ignored. It rarely happens in the ordinary affairs of life that food and drink are not placed first in importance. Seldom if ever does meal time give way to prayer time. "Eat, drink and be merry," is the slogan of this world. In

Nineveh, however, even the beasts, herds and flocks were to be included in a fast. All work was to come to a standstill in order that prayer might be given its proper place. In all the Bible there is no call to prayer as urgent as this one.

The king of Nineveh did not try to persuade his people about the importance of prayer—he simply urged them to pray. It is not what we say or think about prayer that counts, but our actual praying. Many people believe in the importance of prayer, but still do not give themselves to prayer. The king of Nineveh, realizing that the judgment clouds of God's wrath were ready to be poured out, called for immediate prayer. In our day similar judgment clouds are gathering. If an all-out prayer service was needed in Nineveh, it is needed also today. We need to heed the warning of Christ, "Take ye heed, watch and pray: for ye know not when the time is" (Mark 13:33). In other words, stop in your tracks, forget about other things and give prayer its rightful place in your life. "Seek Jehovah while he may be found, call ye upon him while he is near" (Isa. 55:6).

The people of Nineveh were urged to "cry mightily" to God. This was not a time to mumble a few polished sentences and label them prayer. Thorough confessions of sin were needed. The "inward parts" had to be opened and the "hidden parts" exposed (Ps. 51:6). No soul can "cry mightily" unless he means business with God. Hypocrisy and sham must make a quick exit. "Crying mightily" comes only from broken and contrite hearts (Ps. 51:17). It comes from individuals who realize that they have the death sentence hanging over them. It is only such who find the Lord. "Ye shall seek Jehovah thy

God, and thou shalt find him, when thou searchest after him with all thy heart and with all thy soul" (Deut. 4:29).

The people of Nineveh were to pray "to God." What a privilege to have immediate access to the very presence of God! The quickest way to travel is by prayer. Instantly we can be in His presence and make our requests known. The Lord has told us to "draw near with boldness unto the throne of grace, that we may receive mercy, and may find grace to help us in time of need" (Heb. 4:16). One of the greatest thrills on earth should be prayer. To think that we who are so small and weak can make our requests known to a God who is so great and mighty! If the reality of God's presence ever dawned on us, our praying would be different. The two short words, "to God," that concluded the proclamation should never be forgotten. Pray, yes, but pray to God, the Creator of the entire universe.

Anybody who has a need can pray. No doubt the prayers of the people of Nineveh were simple, for they had never been taught how to pray. They were rank heathen. However, when they saw their need and were told to pray, they just prayed. A drowning man never needs to be instructed how to call for help. When he realizes his plight, he just calls out "mightily." Where there is a great enough need, there is also ability to pray. People who say they cannot pray are deceiving themselves. God will never tell us to do something we cannot do. When the Lord admonishes us to "watch and pray," He means that very thing. Some of the greatest prayers in the Bible came from ordinary people with a great need. "Make me clean" cleansed a leper; "Open my eyes" gave sight to the blind; and "God, be thou merciful to me, a sinner" justified a poor publican.

Prayer changed Nineveh. Prayer can change any situation. Jesus said men "ought always to pray and not to faint" (Luke 18:1). If crying mightily to God saved Nineveh, what won't such crying do today?

40

Mercy

"And God saw their works, that they turned from their evil way; and God repented of the evil which he said he would do unto them; and he did it not" (Jonah 3: 10).

The seventh and last step in the Nineveh awakening was the act of mercy that the Lord showed the people. This was by far the most important step. The other steps dealt with the human side of the awakening, but now we consider the divine side. After all, the important part of any awakening is not what human beings do, but what God does. Thus we close the third chapter of Jonah also by beholding the mercy of the Lord.

Mercy and God cannot be separated. When Moses asked for a revelation of God, God introduced Himself as "Jehovah, a God merciful and gracious, slow to anger, and abundant in lovingkindness and truth" (Ex. 34:6). The first attribute mentioned is mercy, though the Lord could have told of many other things instead. The psalmist David affirmed the mercy of God. After he had fallen into sin and had seen himself as a lost and condemned soul, he threw himself on that mercy. "Have mercy upon

142

me, O God" (Ps. 51:1), was his prayer. When the cry was heard, he could bear testimony that the Lord was indeed a merciful God.

Satan does not want us to know God as the "Father of mercies" (II Corinthians 1:3). He would have us believe that God is a hard, severe judge, always ready to condemn, never a God of mercy. But let us look to the Word of God. We read that He is "rich in mercy, for his great love wherewith he loved us" (Eph. 2:4). He has much mercy—enough not only for some occasions, but for every occasion. It is an abundant amount that cannot be exhausted.

God's mercies are tender. Paul wrote to his Philippian friends that he longed for them "in the tender mercies of Christ Jesus" (1:8). Mercies are wonderful, but tender mercies are even more wonderful. All our contacts with Jesus Christ prove that His mercies are tender. How good to know, even though we live in a world that is hard and unsympathetic, that we have a God rich in tender mercies. Truly, "Jehovah is good to all; and his tender mercies are over all his works" (Ps. 145:9). He "crowneth thee with lovingkindness and tender mercies" (Ps. 103: 4). No earthly king ever received a greater crowning than a helpless individual who has been crowned with the lovingkindness and tender mercies of our God.

God saves souls and sends awakenings because of His mercy. It was "not by works done in righteousness which we did ourselves, but according to his MERCY he saved us" (Titus 3:5). Peter writes that it was "according to his great mercy" that "he begat us again unto a living hope" (I Pet. 1:3). Then we can rightfully say that no one knows the Lord as

Saviour unless he has experienced His mercy. We may know about the Lord as creator, provider, sustainer and maker, but such knowledge will not save us. It is when we have accepted His mercy as we find it in Jesus Christ that we really begin to know Him.

Nineveh, a wicked, ungodly city on the verge of destruction, with but forty days of grace remaining, was spared because of God's infinite mercy. When God saw that they turned from their evil way, He withheld the judgment. In speaking of the mercy of God, the writer James expressed it thus: "Mercy glorieth against judgment" (2:13).

God's mercy has not been weakened. It is just as great today as it has been down through the ages. He is "longsuffering to you-ward, not wishing that any should perish, but that all should come to repentance" (II Pet. 3:9). All who are under the wrath of God can, like the people of Nineveh, appeal to His mercy and be saved. This is still the day of grace. Let us learn from the Ninevites, and "cry mightily" to a God who is rich in tender mercy.

41

Anger

*"But it displeased Jonah exceedingly, and he was
angry. . . . And Jehovah said, Doest thou well to
be angry?"* (Jonah 4:1, 4)

An awakening has various effects upon people, for
it touches the entire keyboard of the human heart.
Melodies in both the major and minor keys are
heard. There is joyful harmony bursting forth in
praise and thanksgiving to God for salvation. But
low rumblings of disharmony and discontent are
often present too. The same work of God has different effects upon different people. Some are melted
by His goodness whereas others are hardened by it,
just as butter is melted and clay hardened by the
same sun.

The third chapter introduced us to a people in
Nineveh who were yielding to God; chapter four
reveals Jonah's stubborn heart which is resisting
God. Had the book closed with chapter three, the
ending would have been beautiful. However, there
is something besides the awakening that God would
teach us. We shall note seven lessons in this closing
chapter. First we shall consider the spirit of anger
that dominated Jonah.

It is interesting to see how subtle Satan was in his attack on Jonah. When he was losing his hold on the people of Nineveh, he immediately made a bid for Jonah. How timely the warning of God's Word to all soul winners, "Brethren, even if a man be overtaken in any trespass, ye who are spiritual, restore such a one in a spirit of gentleness; looking to thyself, lest thou also be tempted" (Gal. 6:1). God's servant is warned that in helping others, he himself is apt to be tempted, not necessarily to the sins of the individual he is helping, but to some other more subtle sin. Satan strikes with bitter revenge upon all who are out to proclaim God's message. It is nothing to wonder at that Jonah became a target at this particular time. As he fell into a snare, he became sad when he should have been glad; he became angry with God when he should have been full of praise.

Anger is a mark of the flesh. It is one of the things which proceed out of a man that defile the man (Mark 7:21-23). It springs forth from the fallen nature that was handed down to us by our parents and can be traced back to Adam. It is that nature that is called the flesh, the old man, the old Adam, or the self life. It wants to dominate and control our lives. It has self as its pivot and seeks to make the rest of the world rotate about that center. It is easily hurt and becomes displeased and angry if it does not get its own way. It rebels against God and "is not subject to the law of God, neither indeed can it be" (Rom. 8:7). It tries to exalt itself and always fights against the new life that God gives. "The flesh lusteth against the Spirit, and the Spirit against the flesh; for these are contrary the one to the other"

(Gal. 5:17). The flesh is determined to win and refuses to be held in subjection. At an unguarded moment it takes complete control of us as it did of Jonah. His clannish spirit could not stand to see his enemies spared. He wanted them annihilated as he had prophesied; and when God showed mercy instead, Jonah became displeased and then gave way to anger.

The flesh and Satan are bosom friends. It is always our flesh that opens the heart's door to Satan. When the evil one suspects we are on guard against certain traits of our flesh, he will work on others of which we are less conscious. If he sees he cannot get us to fall for the vulgar works of the flesh such as fornication and drunkenness, he will arouse our flesh on the more subtle sins of jealousy, hate or anger. Satan knows that regardless of which sin we yield to, we simply turn ourselves over to him. Then if we refuse to repent, we have the solemn warning from God that "they who practice such things shall not inherit the kingdom of God" (Gal. 5:21). Therefore Satan would just as soon attack us on the less guarded side of our nature. He is like a champion fisherman: he uses the bait that gets the fish. If an individual is caught easier on the "anger" hook than on the "fornication" hook, he uses the former. Satan is continually changing bait in order to deceive his prey. He is out to get his victim in any possible way. How foolish to refuse our flesh on some points and give in on others. No battle is won that way. An army must stand firm on the entire battle front; for if the enemy breaks through in one place, the cause will be lost.

The sin of anger must be dealt with in the same

way as any other sin. God asked Jonah the pointed question, "Doest thou well to be angry?" Anger can eat away in our hearts like a cancer. The longer it is there, the more harm it does. Its very nature is poisonous. God says, "PUT TO DEATH therefore your members which are upon the earth . . . for which things' sake cometh the wrath of God upon the sons of disobedience . . . put them all away: anger, wrath, malice . . . put off the old man with his doings" (Col. 3:5-9). There is no pussyfooting about God's demands in regard to this sin. He asks that the death penalty be given it. Nothing less will satisfy Him, for "they that are in the flesh cannot please God" (Rom. 8:8). We either deal out the death penalty to our flesh, or our flesh will cause the death penalty to come upon us. "If ye live after the flesh ye must die" (Rom. 8:13). That means eternal death—eternal separation from God.

God has made it clear that all the activities of our fallen nature are sin and must be dealt with as sin. The only possible cure is to confess these sins to Jesus Christ and ask Him for a clean heart. Martin Luther gives sound advice in his catechism: "The old Adam in us is to be drowned and destroyed by daily sorrow and repentance, together with all sins, and evil lusts, and again the new man should daily come forth and rise that shall live in the presence of God in righteousness and purity forever."

This, then, is the way to deal with such a subtle sin as anger. "If we confess our sins, he is faithful and righteous to forgive us our sins and to cleanse us from all unrighteousness" (I John 1:9).

42

The Sitting Prophet

"Then Jonah went out of the city, and sat on the east side of the city" (Jonah 4:5a).

Jonah left the city of Nineveh when the awakening was reaching its zenith. His feelings of prejudice and superiority toward the people of Nineveh had not as yet been subdued. This caused him to give way to his flesh so that he could not bear to remain in a place where God's Spirit was working so mightily. The flesh and the Spirit just cannot get along. There is no place big enough to keep them both, "for the flesh lusteth against the Spirit, and the Spirit against the flesh; for these are contrary the one to the other" (Gal. 5:17). One or the other will have to give way. Therefore Jonah "went out . . . and sat," and left the awakening to take its own course.

The words "went out" well describe an individual who no longer follows the will of the Lord. The Nineveh revival that should have brought great joy to Jonah now caused him to become sour. The mighty moving of God's Spirit in others left him glum and angry, all because he gave way to the flesh. It is a serious offense against God when a person no longer yields to His will. There is nothing God's Spirit can do for such a one as long as he insists on remaining in that state. God's Spirit is not to be harnessed by anyone. It is not the Lord Who is to yield to *us*, but rather we who are to yield to Him.

God's Spirit never anoints one who insists on living in the flesh. Therefore, when we live according to our flesh, we prevent God from anointing us with "the oil of gladness" (Heb. 1:9). Like Jonah we then separate ourselves from the blessings and slump into a sitting position.

Many are the individuals who were once in the midst of God's program but then "went out." Judas finally "went away unto the chief priests." "Demas," Paul writes, "forsook me, having loved this present world." The apostle John tells of a group with the spirit of antichrist that "went out from us . . . they were not of us." Of the disciples who once followed Jesus, we read that "many . . . went back, and walked no more with him." Many more names could be added to this list.

In our own experience we can recall those who were once actively engaged in doing the Lord's work and then suddenly "went out." Satan is no respecter of persons. He will try in subtle ways to influence every Christian to give way to his flesh so that it might be said of him that he "went out."

Jonah not only went out, but we read he "sat." Here sits one of God's chosen messengers absolutely useless. He who was once God's mouthpiece, now has not a word to say. How busy Jonah could have been had he stayed where the Lord had sent him. Jonah who moved thousands when he preached

God's message, now moves no one—not even himself.

Jonah is a type of the person who gets out of God's will. Isolated and lonely, he no longer witnesses the mighty moving of God's Spirit. He accomplishes nothing. No one seems to care for him, and he no longer cares for others. All who sit in this seat are truly miserable.

The demand for a worker was great at this particular time. The newly converted people in Nineveh needed guidance. Who would be more qualified to do this work than Jonah? His training had been along this very line, and yet there he sat useless. The demand may be ever so great and yet God refuses to work through men who are living in the flesh, for "they that are in the flesh cannot please God" (Rom. 8:8).

We also learn from Jonah that no matter how much a person may have been used in the past, he can quickly be set aside. Jonah, who was instrumental in helping thousands of people to get right with God, finally fell from that right relationship with God himself. He had rendered himself useless because he yielded to his old stubborn nature. During the time he was in this state, God had nothing to say to him about service.

SAT is a very characteristic word. All who go out from God's program soon find themselves in a sitting position. Had Jonah been in a right relationship with God at this time, he would have been on his knees in prayer or on his feet preaching.

The apostle Paul had a horror at the thought that he might some day slip out of God's will. Therefore, he writes, "I buffet my body, and bring it into bondage: lest by any means, after that I have preached to others, I myself should be rejected" (I Cor. 9:27). If Paul feared this danger, should not we fear it much more? Let us ask God to help us take to heart the words of Jesus when He said, "Take ye heed, watch and pray" (Mark 13:33).

When Jonah "went out . . . and sat," he was a type of backslider. Many are those who have done likewise. Some once preached the gospel, taught Sunday school classes, acted as deacons and trustees or participated in other phases of Christian work; but they "went out . . . and sat." Today many of them are still sitting. Death will overtake them unless they are aroused soon. May this lesson from Jonah be a means of awakening some such person.

If you recognize yourself in this message, call upon the Lord right where you are sitting. Confess the sins of your heart and tell Him what it was that irked you when you "went out." Throw yourself on His mercy and He will abundantly pardon. Use the words of the prophet, "But as for me, I will look unto Jehovah; I will wait for the God of my salvation: . . . when I fall, I shall arise; when I sit in darkness, Jehovah will be a light unto me" (Micah 7:7, 8).

43

A Passing Joy

"*And Jehovah God prepared a gourd, and made it to come up over Jonah, that it might be a shade over his head, to deliver him from his evil case. So Jonah was exceeding glad because of the gourd*" (Jonah 4:6).

The discouraged Jonah suddenly became "exceeding glad." If we had seen him when circumstances "displeased Jonah exceedingly" and then had seen him when he was "exceeding glad," we would have wondered why the sudden change. We never could have guessed that the reason for this sudden joy was a little bush or tree that had quickly grown up alongside his camping place.

The gourd made Jonah exceeding glad because it was a means of personal comfort to him. He could sit at ease and be concerned only about himself. Since Jonah was now living according to his flesh, we could expect such a reaction. A person who lives according to his old selfish nature can never be happy unless he gains personal advantages. That is why many people rejoice more over personal gain, popularity, friends or a savings account than over eternal things. It is impossible to please a person who lives according to his flesh except by these earthly things. "They that are after the flesh mind the things of the flesh" (Rom. 8:5). The Lord, however, admonishes us to seek "first his kingdom, and his righteousness; and all these things shall be added" (Matt. 6:33). It is so easy to go wrong on this point and, like Jonah, to base our joy on the personal advantages that come our way.

Jonah was still in the flesh even though he was exceeding glad. It is easy to be fooled and think that when a person suddenly comes out of the "blues" he is back on "victory street." But even the devil can make people glad. Most people who drink alcohol get a spirit of frivolity that they do not reveal during their sober moments. Many individuals who are fast heading for eternal punishment are full of laughter. The clowns of our day are not the saints. Even a fool can laugh. "For as the crackling of the thorns under a pot, so is the laughter of the fool" (Eccl. 7:6). There is an experience of being exceeding glad which does not come from God but from outward circumstances.

It is easy, even for a Christian, to have the wrong thing as his greatest joy. When the seventy disciples returned from a preaching mission rejoicing over their success, Jesus quickly admonished them, "Nevertheless in this rejoice not, that the spirits are subject unto you; but rejoice that your names are written in heaven" (Luke 10:20). Jesus wanted them to rejoice in something that was lasting. They were rejoicing over their success; He wanted them to rejoice over *His* success—their eternal salvation. People whose joy is limited to the success that they see in their own work are rapidly heading for disappointment. There are days when God's servants must labor on when the demons are not subject to them, times when there are no visible results. He that limits his joy to what he is able to see can expect some heartaches.

He that has learned to "rejoice in the Lord" (Phil. 3:1) can continue on with his rejoicing even under the most severe testings. In this respect, too, "the righteous shall live by faith" (Gal. 3:11). Many are the Christians whose joy is impoverished because they have not learned to "rejoice in the Lord always" (Phil. 4:4). The Christian's rejoicing can be constant, for the Lord is "the same yesterday and today, yea and for ever" (Heb. 13:8).

It is interesting to see from God's Word what brought joy to the saints of old. The Psalmist said, "I rejoice at thy word, as one that findeth great spoil" (119:162). He also described the righteous man as one who delights in the law of Jehovah and meditates on it day and night (Ps. 1:2). The apostle Paul wrote to the Philippians a letter of joy, rejoicing even though he was a prisoner. The gloomy prison walls and the cold iron chains could not prevent him from being exceeding glad. He had learned "in whatsoever state [he was], therein to be content" (Phil. 4:11). He further wrote, "We also rejoice in our tribulations" (Rom. 5:3), and again, "Now I rejoice in my sufferings for your sake" (Col. 1:24). The apostle James wrote, "Count it all joy, my brethren, when ye fall into manifold temptations; knowing that the proving of your faith worketh patience" (1:2, 3). The apostle John wrote, "Greater joy have I none than this, to hear of my children walking in the truth" (III John 4). Of

Jesus it is written, "Who for the joy that was set before him endured the cross" (Heb. 12:2). How different all this rejoicing is from that of Jonah. These saints of old had anchored their joy in something more substantial than a gourd.

Jonah has ample reason to be ashamed of his source of joy. A mere gourd that had provided shade for his body was all that it took to lift his emotions. If Jonah could be so easily deceived, perhaps it is timely for us to check ourselves. What is it that makes us exceeding glad? What is it that gives us our happiest moments? Do the luxuries, comforts and pleasures of this life determine our greatest joy? Are we by any chance dominated by our subtle flesh so that our exceeding glad moments are caused by the things that are seen? If so, we are guilty of sin. We are no better than Jonah. We are like the people in Amos' day who rejoiced "in a thing of nought" (6:13). Let us confess our sin and pray for grace to "seek the things that are above, where Christ is, seated on the right hand of God," and to set our "mind on the things that are above, not on the things that are upon the earth" (Col. 3:1, 2).

44

Destruction

"But God prepared a worm when the morning rose the next day, and it smote the gourd, that it withered" (Jonah 4:7).

Destruction came from a very insignificant source —just a worm. It was a small slow-moving creature that went about its destructive work quietly and unobserved. We usually pay no attention to such forces until after they have done their damage; then, when it is too late, we become "worm-conscious."

Destruction often comes at a time when we least expect it. It was "when the morning rose," that the worm did its work. Jonah, no doubt, was still deep in sleep when the worm crawled over the spot where he had been sitting when he was so "exceeding glad because of the gourd." It happened in the promising hours of a new day when all the earth was getting ready to stir itself once more. At that innocent moment the worm made its way to the gourd and started to bore into it. Since destruction, like this worm, chooses its own time, we do well to heed the words of Christ, "Take heed to yourself, lest haply your hearts be overcharged with surfeiting, and drunkenness, and cares of this life, and that day come on you suddenly as a snare" (Luke 21:34).

Destruction does not announce its approach. It creeps up unnoticed and goes directly to work. Oftentimes, as in the case of Jonah, a false joy and contentment precede its coming. Belshazzar's hilarious feast was in full progress when the handwriting appeared on the wall, announcing his doom. So also in the last days of this age, "When they are saying, Peace and safety, then sudden destruction cometh upon them, as travail upon a woman with child; and they shall in no wise escape" (I Thess. 5:3). Perhaps at this very moment, as we are rejoicing over various things that we call our own, some destructive forces are at work taking them away from us.

"The next day" revealed the extent of the destruction. One word well described it—"withered." In place of the once promising gourd there stood a withered dead bush, a sad reminder of a yesterday's joy. "The next day" always has a story to tell, and altogether too often it is a sad one. How often people have taken pride in a beautiful home, only to find one day, "when the morning rose," that it had become a smoldering heap of ruins. Others have enjoyed a highly polished automobile and have driven it in pursuit of joy and happiness; but, "when the morning rose" one day, it lay in the ditch, a heap of wreckage. Still others have found their source of greatest joy in some loved one, and their hopes have all been shattered when that one was laid to rest in a freshly dug grave. These sobering examples are a call to think. It is not what we have today that counts, but what we have when the day of eternity dawns. Let us prepare for that day that is coming. "Set your mind on the things that are above, not on the things that are upon the earth" (Col. 3:2).

The earth is full of destructive powers that are continually at work. All material things will sooner or later have to give way to them, "for the things which are seen are temporal; but the things which are not seen are eternal" (II Cor. 4:18). All that is made from the dust of this earth will eventually go back to dust again. "Dust thou art, and unto dust shalt thou return" (Gen. 3:19). There is no material thing that we have in our possession that will not some day be destroyed. The Lord would save us from heartbreaking experiences by warning us, "Love not the world, neither the things that are in the world . . . the world passeth away, and the lust thereof: but he that doeth the will of God abideth forever" (I John 2:15, 17).

We never know how attached we are to earthly things until we have to give them up. Some seemingly good Christians are poor losers. At a time when their testimony could really count, they have none to give. Like Jonah they have become so discouraged that they want to die. Their hearts have been so set on the earthly things they have lost that they refuse to be comforted. This we see especially when some loved one is taken away by death. Some even become bitter against God and lose all interest in living. The great Bible character Job was quite different; he knew how to meet a loss. The day he lost his ten children and all his wealth, he made the memorable statement, "Jehovah gave, and Jehovah hath taken away; blessed be the name of Jehovah" (1:21).

Prepare for the death worms. They are busy

crawling here and there, smiting one thing after another. Like a mighty, unconquered army they leave a "withered" trail behind them. Their approach cannot be stopped. In time they will have gnawed their way into the heart of every earthly thing. Most people will suffer a complete loss; but others, like Mary who sat at Jesus' feet, have "chosen the good part, which shall not be taken away" (Luke 10:42). Jesus offers to all those who become His disciples a joy that "no one taketh away from you" (John 16:22)—no, not even all this world's destructive powers combined!

45

Thoughts on Death

"Jonah . . . requested for himself that he might die, and said, It is better for me to die than to live" (Jonah 4:8).

Death is a sobering subject. Everyone thinks of it at times, for every day brings direct or indirect reminders of it. Sometimes we wonder WHEN death will come, whether in youth, middle age or old age. Then again we wonder HOW death will come—perhaps through sickness or accident. WHERE shall we meet it—in our own home, in a hospital, on the battle field, at some scene of accident on land or sea? Shall we have a premonition of its approach so we can make special preparations, or shall we meet it unannounced? Shall we suffer long before it comes, or shall we be in good health? Shall we outlive our loved ones, or will our time of departure come first? These and similar questions race through our minds when we think of death.

Death is appointed for all. Each year when I get my appointment book, I first copy the words, "It is appointed unto men once to die, and after this cometh judgment" (Heb. 9:27). Not knowing what year this appointment will take place, I think it well to write it in each year's book. This is one appointment that God has made for us, and no excuse on our part can change it. The appointed time will be kept to within a split second. Regardless of how slothful we have been with other appointments, this is one that we shall keep. The saint and the wicked alike will face this sober moment. Old or young, wealthy or poor, black or white—it makes no difference, for death is no respecter of persons.

A Christian need not fear death. "When Christ died, he brought to nought him that had the power of death, that is, the devil: and delivered all them who through fear of death were all their lifetime subject to bondage" (Heb. 2:14, 15). The fear of death is one of the worst kinds of bondage. It can haunt a poor soul day and night throughout his life. Christ came to remove this fear, being ordained by God to "taste of death for every man" (Heb. 2:9). When Christ arose from the grave, He burst asunder the shackles of death and proclaimed victory over it. "If we have become united with him in the likeness of his death, we shall be also in the likeness of his resurrection" (Rom. 6:5). Death will have no more power over a Christian than it had over Christ. "As in Adam all die, so also in Christ shall all be made alive. But each in his own order: Christ the first-fruits; then they that are Christ's, at his coming" (I Cor. 15:22, 23). All Christians can now claim in Christ the victory over the fear of death. With the Psalmist all true believers can say, "Yea, though I walk through the valley of the shadow of death, I will fear no evil; for thou art with me" (23:4).

Jonah's motive for wanting to die was wrong. In

his sore disappointment, he longed to get away from everything instead of dealing with his stubborn nature. This is another subtle temptation of the evil one. Often when a person doesn't get his own way, he feels sorry for himself. He is then tempted to believe that death would be a relief. Such thoughts are wrong; one with this spirit is not ready for death. He is guilty of mental cowardice, trying to evade the issue before him. Sometimes in a moment of weakness, a sorely tempted one will try to win his point by referring to his own death, threatening that "You will be sorry after I am dead and gone." No advantage is ever gained by this kind of reasoning. It is just the flesh trying desperately to get its own way. Some who yield on this point will continue going until they even commit suicide. Our flesh is not to be toyed with. The sooner we confess such thoughts and words as sin, the sooner we shall be free to continue our lives as God has planned them.

There is a longing for death that is right. A true child of God feels like a stranger and a pilgrim here. He realizes that earth is not his home and that all its possessions are temporal. He longs for the day when his pilgrimage will be over, so that he can forever be with the Lord. Like Paul he says, "For to me to live is Christ, and to die is gain. I am in a strait betwixt the two, having the desire to depart and be with Christ; for it is very far better: yet to abide in the flesh is more needful for your sake" (Phil. 1:21-24).

Many dear saints who feel that their life's work is over are permitted to stay on earth yet longer, so they can give themselves to a prayer ministry. In this last work, they often experience an intense longing to be with Christ in heaven. Most of their friends have already gone, and they are eager to join them. They crave relief from the warfare against the devil, the world and their own flesh—these enemies which have raged furiously for so many years. Such longings are pleasing to God and are altogether different from those experienced by Jonah.

Another truth we must not overlook when thinking about death is the truth about the return of Christ to this earth. There is a possibility that some Christians who read these lines will not meet with death. On the day that Christ returns He "himself shall descend from heaven, with a shout, with the voice of the archangel, and with the trump of God: and the dead in Christ shall rise first; then we that are alive, that are left, shall together with them be caught up in the clouds, to meet the Lord in the air: and so shall we ever be with the Lord. Wherefore comfort one another with these words" (I Thess. 4:16, 17). The return of the Lord has been the hope of Christians down through the ages. The crown of righteousness is promised to those who have loved His appearing. We are no doubt very close to that great day. If it comes before we die, we shall be the privileged people who will be caught up to meet the Lord in the air. What a glorious day that will be. Does it not thrill your heart just to think of it? We are admonished to comfort one another with these words.

Death—or the sudden return of the Lord—is soon upon us. It may be only a matter of days before that great event will take place. The day and the hour knoweth no man so we leave that with our heavenly

Father. But we should live every day as if it were the last. What better conclusion could we come to on this subject than to listen again to the warning of Christ, "Watch therefore: for ye know not on what day your Lord cometh" (Matt. 24:42). "Take ye heed, watch and pray: for ye know not when the time is" (Mark 13:33). "What I say unto you I say unto all, Watch" (Mark 13:37).

46

Children

"Should not I have regard for Nineveh, that great city, wherein are more than sixscore thousand persons that cannot discern between their right hand and their left hand; and also much cattle?" (Jonah 4:11).

God has always been interested in children. He shows it again by the above words. The "sixscore thousand persons that cannot discern between their right hand and their left hand" were small children —one hundred twenty thousand in all. These were a host of helpless little infants entombed in godless homes scattered throughout Nineveh. It was for their sakes that God would have regard for the city.

It is interesting to notice that of all the people living in Nineveh, God referred just to this one group of helpless infants. He had nothing to say about the old folks, the middle-aged or even the young people. Not even the king and his nobles who cried so mightily to God for mercy were given any recognition. It was rather because of the babies that God would have regard for Nineveh. God knew the possibilities in these one hundred twenty thousand heathen infants. They each had a precious soul that was worth more than the combined wealth of the world. Within their ranks was a potential Peter, Paul, John or James. The hope of Nineveh was to be found among the children if only they were given a chance. Therefore the fatherly eye of God was tenderly watching over them. This was another case where "God chose the weak things of the world, that he might put to shame the things that are strong" (I Cor. 1:27).

The little children of Nineveh were a greater blessing to their parents and neighbors than anyone realized. It is easy to overlook little children just because they cannot work and accomplish great things. Jesus once said, "Whosoever shall receive one of such little children in my name, receiveth me" (Mark 9: 37). This is a startling statement, and should cause us to think. At another time when the disciples asked Jesus who was the greatest in the kingdom of heaven "he called to him a little child . . . and said, Verily I say unto you, Except ye turn, and become as little children, ye shall in no wise enter into the kingdom of heaven" (Matt. 18:2, 3). I am sure the disciples gasped when this statement was made. Children are indeed a blessing in more than one way, and there is much we can learn from them.

We are interested especially in the young people of our day, for in them we see great possibilities. Our God would teach us that we need to be interested first in the infant group. If we ignore the little children, we shall never be able to handle them when they reach their teens. We are told that a child learns more the first few years of his life than at any other time, and we are making a sad mistake by ignoring this age group. God's Word says, "Train up a child in the way he should go, and even when he is old he will not depart from it" (Prov. 22:6). This training is to begin at the day of the child's birth. We should regard little children not only as the church of tomorrow, but as a vital part of the church of today.

Children are often the ones that God uses to further His purposes. The history of many a church reveals that it was begun with a small Sunday school in the community. From this seemingly insignificant beginning a strong congregation was later established. Many parents can also testify that they were won for Christ and His church through their children. The influence of the Sunday school was used to draw the parents to the church. In other cases God has taken a little child to Himself by death in order to make the parents eternity-minded. These and similar instances are times when "a little child shall lead them." Heaven's book will some day reveal some interesting facts along this line.

The most beautiful faith on earth is found in the heart of a saved child. A child is much more receptive to the Word of God than anyone else. Jesus said of these little ones, "Suffer the little children to come unto me, and forbid them not: for to such belongeth the kingdom of God" (Luke 18:16). These words of Jesus stand as a memorial for all children of all times. The kingdom of God belongs to them. Is it not sad that so many little children in our day are trapped in ungodly homes? What could not be done for them—the most helpless of all people, and yet the most receptive to the gospel—if they were given a chance?

Woe to anyone who mistreats a child! Children

are under the guiding care of angels. "See that ye despise not one of these little ones: for I say unto you, that in heaven their angels do always behold the face of my Father who is in heaven" (Matt. 18: 10). To offend a child means to offend God. "Whoso shall cause one of these little ones that believe on me to stumble, it is profitable for him that a great millstone should be hanged about his neck, and that he should be sunk in the depth of the sea" (Matt. 18: 6). He who handles children is handling God's jewels.

It is a serious thing to neglect children. If their hearts are not turned to God, they will grow up to become champions for evil. Evidently Jonah and his people did nothing to follow up the awakening. Jonah's prophecy took place during the reign of Jeroboam II, about 781-740 B.C. Israel fell captive to the Assyrians in 722 B.C. Then it is probable that some of the infants who are here referred to made up a part of the victorious army which later overcame Israel and led them as slaves into Assyria. If so, these seemingly insignificant infants later became the masters of Israel.

Jonah had forgotten all about the little children. He was so politically minded that all he desired was that God would hurl an "atomic bomb" at Nineveh and annihilate everyone. Then he and his people Israel would have been forever free from their bitter enemy, the Assyrians. Imagine how Jonah must have felt when God reminded him of the "sixscore thousand persons" to whom he had not given a thought. No wonder Jonah was struck speechless and had nothing to answer the Lord. The book ends on this abrupt note, for the last word worth recording had been spoken.

Jonah no doubt packed up soon after this and went home a wiser man. As he trudged along mile after mile, he had plenty to think about. When he came to Nineveh, he had been conscious of a multitude of ruthless soldiers who had continually molested his people; when he returned, his mind was occupied with another multitude—the one hundred and twenty thousand who made up the infant population of Nineveh. God had to send Jonah all the way to Nineveh to make him child-conscious. I wonder what God will have to do with some of us before we learn this lesson.

47

The Question Mark

"Should not I have regard for Nineveh, that great city, wherein are more than sixscore thousand persons that cannot discern between their right hand and their left hand; and also much cattle?" (Jonah 4:11).

The book of Jonah ends with a question mark. There is a reason for this, and we shall draw a few parting lessons from it.

The Lord never asks a question unless it is important. We do well, then, to ponder His questions and seek their right answers. From the first question addressed to Adam, "Where art thou?" (Gen. 3:9) to the last one found in the Bible, we could have a rich Bible study in itself. In the book of Jonah there are three questions: "Doest thou well to be angry? (4:4), "Doest thou well to be angry for the gourd?" (4:9) and the text we are now considering, "Should not I have regard for Nineveh?" Jonah made no attempt to answer the first of these questions; to the second he blurted out the rebellious answer, "I do well to be angry, even unto death"; the final question left him tongue-tied. The Lord's questions are all pointed and find their way deep into our hearts.

The question that should concern us now is not what happened to Jonah but rather what is happening to us; not whether Jonah repented but whether we repent; not whether Jonah was saved but whether we are saved. In due time we shall be able to find out what happened to him, but right now our attention should be focused on ourselves. We have been handling the Scriptures and that is a serious matter, for "every scripture inspired of God is also profitable for teaching, for reproof, for correction, for instruction which is in righteousness" (II Tim. 3:16). In other words, God expects action in response to His Word, for "not the hearers of the law are just before God, but the doers of the law shall be justified" (Rom. 2:13). It is easy to hear and read God's Word and then do as the man James wrote about, who "goeth away, and straightway forgetteth what manner of man he was" (1: 24). But to him who is "not a hearer that forgetteth but a doer that worketh, this man shall be blessed in his doing" (v. 25). Jesus said, "If ye know these things, blessed are ye if ye do them" (John 13:17). The all-important question in our minds as we come to the close of this book should be, what is our own response.

The fact that this closing question was not answered would seem to be a good sign. Jonah had been struck speechless as he stood face to face with the infinite love of God. He was, no doubt, so convicted of his own sinfulness that he had nothing to say. Anyone who will honestly face God and investigate His love as it is revealed in the Bible will also become speechless. It is God's purpose "that every mouth may be stopped" (Rom. 3:19). God's law has not done its work until it has caused the sinner to have nothing more to say in his defense. Such silence is indeed golden, for it prepares an atmosphere for God's blessings. It is in the stillness of such moments that heaven's blessings can descend like dew upon a feverish sinner to cool and refresh him. May the Lord's heart-searching questions cause many such moments of silence in these days.

The book ends with our attention focused upon the Lord. He is the all-important one after all. Our attention is fixed on the Lord, where it belongs, rather than on a weak, unstable human being like Jonah. He who would be blessed must rivet his attention on the Lord and not the messenger involved. When a servant of God succeeds in getting his listeners to do this, the sooner he gets out of the way the better. This Philip the evangelist did, when he led the Ethiopian eunuch to salvation. We read that as soon as he had finished his mission, "the Spirit of the Lord caught away Philip; and the eunuch saw him no more" (Acts 8:39). After John the Baptist pointed to Christ and said, "Behold, the Lamb of God, that taketh away the sin of the world!" (John 1:29), his disciples left him and followed Christ. Later John added these memorable words, "He must increase, but I must decrease" (3:30). It seems that Jonah did a similar thing. As we have been gazing at the matchless love of God, as we have beheld him in this last verse of the book, Jonah makes a quick getaway and fades out of the picture. This is indeed a requisite of a good preacher.

The last impression that this book leaves with us is that the Lord is merciful. He is exactly what Jonah testified: "a gracious God, and merciful, slow to anger, and abundant in lovingkindness" (4:2). As we review the previous chapters, we notice that each one closes by revealing God's love. Chapter one closes with Jehovah creating a great fish to save Jonah; chapter two closes by again revealing the Lord's love when Jonah was delivered from the fish upon dry land; chapter three closes by revealing the Lord's love when He spared the people of Nineveh; and chapter four closes the book with a further revelation of the Lord's infinite love when He spared Nineveh for the sake of the helpless children and cattle. Thus each chapter climaxed itself in God's love. If we were to characterize the Lord from our study of Him in this book, we could well do so in the words of I John 4:8, "God is love."

With our eyes upon the Lord and with the significant words, "God is love," ringing in our hearts, we bring our series of meditations to a close. We have come to the parting of the ways. Before we part, may the final words be those of Jesus Christ, the Friend of sinners, Who gave Himself up for our sins. "If ye keep my commandments, ye shall abide in my love; even as I have kept my Father's commandments, and abide in his love. These things have I spoken unto you, that my joy may be in you, and that your joy may be made full" (John 15: 10, 11).